The Author's Holy Trinity of Wealth
ACTION • THOUGHT • FAITH

KIM STAFLUND

The Author's Holy Trinity of Wealth
ACTION • THOUGHT • FAITH

From the author who brought us:

How to Publish a Book in the East That You Can Sell in the West in which
"The author has used the simplest words which can be read and understood by everyone. The stepwise information makes this book seamless and interesting."
by Sheetal Maurya, Godse (Halo of Books)

Successful Selling Tips for Introverted Authors proclaimed
"…a 'must-have' for every author. Highly recommended."
by Wisconsin Bookwatch

How to Publish a Bestselling Book touted as
"…exceptional, practical, detailed, comprehensive, and thoroughly 'user friendly' from beginning to end."
by Midwest Book Review

How to Publish a Book in Canada recommended as
"A good source for writers of all experience levels seeking to publish quality books in Canada."
by Kirkus Reviews

KIM STAFLUND
Polished Publishing Group (PPG)

The Author's Holy Trinity of Wealth: ACTION * THOUGHT * FAITH
Ebook ISBN: 978-1-988971-40-7
Paperback ISBN: 978-1-988971-41-4
© 2019 by Kim Staflund

PolishedPublishingGroup

No portion of this book may be duplicated or used in any form, by any electronic or mechanical means (including printing, photocopying, recording, or information storage and retrieval), for any profit-driven enterprise, without prior permission in writing from the publisher. Brief excerpts may be shared subject to inclusion of this copyright notice: © 2019 by Kim Staflund. All rights reserved.

Due to the dynamic nature of the Internet, any website addresses mentioned within this book might have been changed or discontinued since its publication.

For writers, authors, creators:

"Failure is success in progress."
~Albert Einstein

TABLE OF CONTENTS

- INTRODUCTION 15
- ACTION: THE AUTHOR'S MONEY TREE 18
  - The Author's Money Tree Season #1: Planting.......... 18
  - The Author's Money Tree Season #2: Growing 18
  - The Author's Money Tree Season #3: Harvesting 19
  - Even James Patterson Shakes The Author's Money Tree 19
  - This Program Can Work for Fiction, Non-Fiction, and Poetry 21
  - How Do I Know This Works? 24
    - Burnout and Refocus Time...................................... 24
    - Sell More Earn More in the United Kingdom......... 25
    - Sell More Earn More in the United States 26
    - Sell More Earn More in Australia 27
    - Sell More Earn More in Canada ... and All Over the World! 27
- The Author's Money Tree Season #1: Planting............. 29
  - The Power of Google in Helping You Sell Books 29
  - It All Starts with a Book and a Blog 32
  - Why is a Blog Better for Authors than a Regular Website? 33
    - Website vs. Blog: Apple vs. Orange 33
    - Website vs. Blog: Summary 34
  - Keywords are the Seeds That Will Grow Your Readership 35

Keyword Research is Crucial to Your Success 35
How to Know Which Keywords Will Send Quality Traffic to Your Website 36
How to "Borrow" Keyword Research from Other High-Ranking Authors in Your Genre 37
Different Types of Keywords Bring Different Results 37
What's the Difference Between Tags and Keywords? 39
What Search Engines are Looking For 39
The Author's Money Tree Season #2: Growing 40
10 Easy Ways to Fertilize and Insulate Your Crop 40
SEO-Friendly Flesch Reading Ease Score (FRES) 49
Why I Now Use the Free Yoast SEO WordPress Plug-In 50
Your Blog Posts Can Be 300+ Words Long 50
10 Easy Author Blog Post Ideas 51
5 Author Blog Post Ideas About You and Your Books 51
5 Author Blog Post Ideas About Other People or Places 52
What Does it Mean to Monetize Your Blog? 53
Set up an Affiliate Account Through Amazon Associates 54
Set Up a Google AdSense Account 54
The Value of Guest Blogging 55
When You Guest Post on Someone Else's Blog 56
When Someone Else Guest Posts on Your Blog ... 59

What is Content Syndication? 59
   An SEO Analogy: Retail Merchandising 60
   Don't Get Dinged by The SEO Gods! 61
   Content Syndication to The Rescue 62
   Finding the Right Content Syndication Partners for You 63
      Free Syndication Options (Sprint) 63
      Free Syndication Options (Marathon) 67
   How Book Publicists Can Help You Score Guest Blogging and Content Syndication Opportunities with High-Ranking Publications 69
      Six Important Questions to Ask a Book Publicist .. 72

The Author's Money Tree Season #3: Harvesting 74
   Engage with Your Readers in a More Personal Way. 74
   What is the Difference Between Blog Subscribers versus Registered Users? 78
   Add *This* to Blogging and Watch Your Book Sales Soar Even Higher 82

THOUGHT: THE AUTHOR'S GOLD RUSH 90
   Information is Your Gold Rush 90
   Entertainment is Your Gold Rush 91
   Relationships are Your Gold Rush 91
   The Digital Gold Rush 92
   Three Feet from Gold 93
   Your Simple Business System 96
   How to Further Build Your Readership ... in Your Sleep 96

- Hook Them with an Enticing Opt-In Page 97
- Engage Them with a Special Offer 98
- Manage Them with an Autoresponder 99
- KISS: Keep It Simple, Silly! 100

Primary Components of an Autoresponder 103
- Email Lists/Audience 103
  - List/Audience Name and Defaults 103
  - Required Email Footer Content 107
  - Google Analytics on Archive and List Pages 108
- Create Additional Subscriber Signup Forms 108
  - Form Builder 108
  - Embedded Forms 109
  - Subscriber Pop-ups 111
- Create Email Campaigns to Engage with Your Readers 111
  - Broadcast Emails (A Monthly Newsletter) 112
  - Automated Emails (Share Your Blog Posts) 114
  - PPC Ad Campaigns (Facebook/Instagram and Google) 116
  - Landing Page 119

Supersize Me! 120
- Would You Like Fries with That? 122
  - Vary Your Automated Blog Post Notifications ... 122
  - Set Up Five Automated Backlist Emails 124
  - Invite Subscribers to Become Your Affiliate Marketers 125

Invite Subscribers to Become Your BETA Readers 128

The Psychology of Email Marketing 130

Scale It Larger by Reinvesting 132

FAITH: THE AUTHOR'S MAGIC KEY 136

The Magic Key to Faith 136

The Magic Key to Focus 136

The Magic Key to Endurance 137

It All Starts with a Clear Vision 138

Is a Lack of Vision Holding *You* Back? 138

Take a Chance on Faith 139

Let These People Inspire You to Build Your Own Clear Vision 140

Her "Idea Moment" Came to Her Before the Actual Idea 140

His Blueprint to Success Was Laid Out for Him in a Magazine Article 141

This Man Dubbed His Calling "The Church of Freedom from Concern" 142

She Just Didn't Want to Live *This* Way Anymore 144

This Woman Asked God to Give Her a Platform to Do Good 145

He Wanted to Help Other People Escape and Feel Inspired 146

My Own Vision Has Always Been About Travel and Freedom 147

What is *Your* Vision? 148

When You Come Up Against Resistance, Stay the Course ... 150

Her Lawyer Thought Her Idea Was *So* Bad, He Must Be on Candid Camera ... 151

This Young Man Was Thrown in Jail for Pursuing His Goal ... 153

This Undiagnosed Dyslexic Started Out Earning Only $25 Per Set ... 156

Her Teachers Were Mentally Abusive and Her Family Resented Her ... 157

Her College Peers Were Jealous of Her Success and Taunted Her About It ... 159

This Italian Actor Couldn't Even Get Cast for a Bit Part ... as an *Italian* ... 161

I Went to the Edge of the Cliff ... and It Crumbled Out from Under Me ... 163

What Are You Telling Yourself About *Your* Obstacles? ... 167

How Much Time Will it Take? ... 169

It Took a Little Over Two Years for Her Invention to be Recognized Nationally ... 169

His First Goal Took Six Years to Achieve and His Second Took 12 ... 170

He Attracted $10,000,000 to Himself Within Three Years ... 171

She Grew Her Bank Account from $11.42 to $62,500 in Three and a Half Years ... 172

It Took Her One Decade to Turn Her Dream into Reality ... 173

He Lived in Poverty for Eight Years Until His Big Break Came 173

It Has Taken Me 25 Years of Trial and Error to Write This Book 173

How Long Will It Take You? 175

Success Leaves Clues (Work Ethic and Sleep Habits) .. 176

She Spent *Countless* Hours on the Road Promoting Her Brand 178

This Man Says "Sleep Faster" to Those Who Think They Need Eight Hours 180

He Worked All Day and Well into the Night for Weeks on End 180

This Single Parent Found a Way to Ensure Her Son's Bright Future 181

This Woman Feels Most Comfortable Working 14 to 16 Hours Per Day 183

His Three-Day Writing Frenzy Earned $200,000,000 184

She Danced Her Way to Becoming the Most Watched Woman in the World 184

His Legacy Is the Epitome of Greatness 186

Writing During His Commute Earned This Author $450,000 in One Year 188

Her Frenzy of Focused Activity Precipitated Million-dollar Book Sales 189

Sleep Doesn't Create Energy. *Faith* Does. 190

I Have Far More Energy Due to This Change in my Sleeping Habits 192

Recommended Resources on Sleep Habits 193
It's Time to Make *Your* Dream Come True 195
Bibliography 197
Index 202
About the Author 206

INTRODUCTION

There is a season to sow, and there is a season to reap ... but you can't do both in the same season. That's why you need both seasons.

For an artist—*any* artist—there is so much more to wealth than financial prosperity. True, holistic wealth is about having the time and freedom to create one's art at will, for the pure enjoyment of it.

Why do writers write? There are varying reasons from the basic desire to share ideas with others to the simple joy of the act itself. I'm one of those writers who does it because I enjoy it. I always have. Since the day I learned how to write, I've been writing in some way, shape, or form. When my high school friends went off to cheerleading practice, soccer, or music lessons after school, I went home to write. Every single day. So, this has never been a chore for me. It's always been my love and passion. If I never earned a dime from it, I would still write every day.

In his article titled "Why Do Writers Write?" on the Psychology Today website, author Lawrence R. Samuel ponders:

> With rejection and criticism so much a part of the literary experience (and the fact that the income of the average American writer hovers around the poverty line), one has to wonder if writers have at least a streak of masochism in their genetic makeup to choose it as their profession. (Samuel, 2018)

This belief that most writers are doomed to a life of poverty seems to be the consensus among writers and non-writers everywhere. I think it is one of the top fears that prevent most "closet authors" from coming out to share their work with others. They may wonder, "What's the point?" and opt for other seemingly more lucrative careers than bother with publishing a book.

But what if I told you times are changing? What if I told you that more and more authors are proving you can, indeed, earn a decent living from writing? I've done much research on this topic matter over the past two years. You can imagine how thrilled I was to learn that it *is* possible.

You may write fiction, non-fiction, or poetry. Or, you may be an author who paid a ghostwriter to do that writing for you. Whoever you are, the information contained here can help you to not only sell your books, but also earn a decent living from them. If holistic wealth as an author is what you're after, there are three necessary steps toward achieving that goal: action, thought, and faith. These components are each covered in depth inside this book. When you reach the end, you will know with certainty that this *is* possible. You'll also know exactly how to achieve it.

ACTION
The Author's Money Tree: How to Grow a Bountiful Readership Organically

"There is nothing to writing. All you do is sit down at a typewriter and bleed."
~Ernest Hemingway

Whether you self-publish or sign with a traditional publisher, you'll need a fan base (a.k.a. platform) of willing buyers to sell your books to. Here's your action plan to build that fan base—a plan that some of today's top authors are using to earn six-figure incomes.

ACTION: THE AUTHOR'S MONEY TREE

It takes three full seasons to reap the *true* rewards of The Author's Money Tree: planting, growing, and harvesting. And it's well worth all the effort.

The Author's Money Tree Season #1: Planting

There are three effective ways to plant an abundance of seeds with your desired readership: productive blogging, prolific publishing, or (better yet) *both*. If you are strategic in the way you do these things, you'll be amazed by how quickly your sprouts begin to show.

That's the beauty of being a writer in this digital age of book publishing. Writing *is* selling in the online world. And keywords are the seeds you're planting to feed all your hungry readers at harvest time.

The Author's Money Tree Season #2: Growing

But those keywords will never be enough on their own. Each sprout needs to be fed and watered so it can grow, and this takes time and patience. Quality content is the fertilizer that breathes life into a sprout and helps it grow into a healthy sapling. Proper search engine optimization (SEO) is the mulch that prevents your sapling from being taken over by larger weeds.

You need a strong root system to grow a bountiful money tree that will bear fruit for you, year after year, and stand the test of time. This is crucial to your progressive success in future harvest seasons, and I'll show you exactly how to do it.

The Author's Money Tree Season #3: Harvesting

And now comes the fun part! Harvest time is when you reap the rewards of all your efforts.

In this section, you'll meet some authors who are earning six-figure incomes from their readerships in their own harvest seasons. You'll learn some of the strategies they're using to harvest the same crops, over and over again, while planting new seeds each year.

Do you want to grow an abundant readership? This is a totally sustainable system that you can use successfully for fiction, non-fiction, and even poetry. Truth!

Even James Patterson Shakes The Author's Money Tree

Independent authors aren't the only ones shaking The Author's Money Tree in new ways. Even mainstream thriller author, James Patterson, has jumped on this band wagon with his BookShots line.

His reason for publishing books this way may be a bit different than the rest of us, as indicated in *The New York Times* article by Alexandra Alter titled "James Patterson Has a Big Plan for Small Books." After all, he doesn't need the money. But no matter who you are, the results are still the same.

> ...Mr. Patterson is after an even bigger audience. He wants to sell books to people who have abandoned reading for television, video games, movies and social media.

> So how do you sell books to somebody who doesn't normally read?
>
> Mr. Patterson's plan: make them shorter, cheaper, more plot-driven and more widely available.
>
> ...He aims to release two to four books a month through Little, Brown, his publisher. All of the titles will be shorter than 150 pages, the length of a novella. (Alter, 2016)

This is one of the greatest keys to success as an author in this day and age: prolific publishing. The single best way to sell books (and build a blog) is to utilize the power of search engines. Ping their algorithms by feeding them new content on a consistent basis. Do this, and they'll reward you by feeding you more traffic. It works the same for Kobo or Amazon's internal search engines as it does for Google, Baidu, Yahoo, or Bing.

But don't let high writing volumes scare you away. This is an entirely achievable plan—even for those of you still working full-time elsewhere while writing part-time on the side. You can still be *you* with the core aspects of your writing. Does this sound familiar?

> Some authors set aside a certain number of hours every day for writing, or a certain number of words. In short, a writing schedule.
>
> Then there's me. No writing for three or six months, then a flurry of activity where I forget to eat, sleep, bathe, change the cat's litter... I'm a walking stereotype. To assuage the guilt, I tell myself that my unconscious is hard at work. As

Hemingway would say, long periods of thinking and short periods of writing. (LaRocca, 2019)

Well, in this book, I'm going to teach you how to take full advantage of "the writing flurries" when they happen. And, once you see the kind of results this program can bring, you may find those flurries increase naturally for you. That's what happened to me. In 2017 and 2018, I wrote and published 35 books and dozens of blog posts to go along with them. It's like the more I wrote, the more my creativity seemed to grow. But I refer you back to James Patterson's BookShots line again. Remember that he's writing *novellas*—not yesterday's idea of an "acceptable" full-length novel. And your blog posts? More good news: these no longer have to be 500+ words long to be effective, either. Even as few as 300 words can still constitute quality content in Google's eyes—so long as the post is set up properly. I'll show you how to blog productively yet efficiently in this book. You won't believe how easy this is!

This Program Can Work for Fiction, Non-Fiction, and Poetry

You could be in any room chatting with your family members, friends, or business colleagues. It doesn't matter where it is or who you're with. At some point during the conversation, a question of some sort almost always arises; what's the first thing everyone does? You each pull out your smartphone, iPad, or tablet and open the web browser to search for an answer to that question. We all have instant access to timely information at our fingertips now, and we're all *constantly* accessing it. Anik Singal, email marketer extraordinaire, says it best with this statement:

> Consider this: Twenty years ago if you wanted to learn something, you'd go to the library or bookstore and pick up a book. If there was new information on a topic, it had to go through a long publication process - an average of 18 months! By the time that new information came out, it was often already outdated.
>
> Today is very different.
>
> We live in the Information Age. Basically, the greatest industry in the world today is the information industry. Those with access to information and the ability to distribute it the fastest are the ones who are poised to be our next millionaires and billionaires. (Singal, 2016)

Now let's take that a step further. As an author, it's not only about your ability to quickly distribute information to the masses that could potentially earn you thousands—even millions—of dollars; it's more about your ability to use that information to connect people together in meaningful ways. Intellectual property—information in the form of patented, trademarked, and copyrighted collections of ideas and concepts—can be priceless assets to the owners who know how to do this well.

> In discussions with industry leaders like Seth Godin and Clay Hebert (among many others), it has become clear that we are in a Connection Economy. The connection economy rewards value created by building relationships and creating connections, rather than building assets by

industrialism. This means the most valuable companies will connect buyer to seller, or consumer to content. If you don't buy that argument, consider these facts:

1. Uber is the largest "taxi" company - yet they own no vehicles and excel at connecting riders with drivers.

2. AirBnB is the largest provider of accommodations - yet they own no real estate.

3. Facebook is the largest media company - yet they create no content.

4. Crowdfunding businesses like Kickstarter and IndiGoGo [sic] are expected to surpass venture capital for funding in 2016 - yet they have no funds to invest.

Whereas it used to be sufficient to sell a product and receive revenues, customers now seek to connect with other like-minded individuals to get the most value in the long run. (Altman, 2015)

Authors can create these kinds of meaningful connections through books. Whether you're a fiction author dedicated to entertaining readers within a certain genre or a non-fiction subject matter expert (SME) who writes how-to or self-help materials, there are umpteen unique ways for you to bond with your readers while uniting them with additional people/resources that can enhance their reading experience. I'll show you some great ways to do this in chapter two of this section, when we take a look at some easy blog post ideas together.

And poets? You have a choice: you can sell your work the way a fiction novelist does; or you can sell it the way a non-fiction SME does. There is a larger market for your poems than simply people who read poetry books for the sake of poetry. Just think about all the instances where poetry can be useful: in greeting cards; on motivational artwork for homes or offices; for obituaries; for special event speeches or presentations; et cetera. Poetry appeals to each reader's emotions in a different way than fiction and non-fiction does. But how you sell it is much the same, believe it or not.

How Do I Know This Works?

My shift in thinking began in around mid-to-late 2015. I had been in the book publishing business, in one capacity or another, for close to 25 years. I'd been publishing books under my own label, Polished Publishing Group (PPG), since November 2009. I knew how to produce a truly professional product for my authors, and I had ample experience to be able to teach them all the traditional book sales and marketing methods. I was a bestselling author in my own right, and so were many of my authors. So, everything looked great on the surface.

But here was the reality: my company wasn't generating enough profit to allow me to leave my full-time sales job. My own royalties, and my best authors' royalties, weren't all that impressive. All these bestsellers were earning less than $500 per year in royalties. That was the hard truth. (Sound familiar? I'll bet it does.)

Burnout and Refocus Time

I was burning out. I could no longer maintain my pace of 50+ hours of corporate sales coupled with another 20+

hours of book publishing, sales, and marketing every week. Especially if there was no end in sight to all this work—no definite increase in profits to show me I was on the right track. I felt discouraged. I felt like I was failing my authors, never mind myself.

So, do you want to know what I did? I quit my full-time job, and I scaled back the publishing work for a little while. There was something I had wanted to do since my early twenties that I allowed myself to do in my forties. I embarked on my very own "Eat, Pray, Love" working holiday in Asia and taught English in Bangkok, Thailand, in 2016. What a blessing this experience was! I was blessed not only by all the people I met and all the life lessons I learned, but also by my renewed sense of purpose when I returned home.

If you're feeling burned out in any way, I recommend you do something like this for yourself. Walk away from your work for a while. Have fun! Eat! Pray! Love! Then, once you're fully rejuvenated, get back to work. You'll be so much more productive if you do. And you may just find the answers to your questions that had eluded you for so long. That's what happened to me.

Sell More Earn More in the United Kingdom

I didn't go back to a "real job" straightaway because I wanted to turn off the corporate noise for a while and *really* focus on my craft. I found four personal investors to help me cover my expenses while I focused. In early 2017, I started studying and learning all about email marketing. I also Googled things like "successful authors" and "profitable publishing" to figure out how to take things to the next level and start making some *real* money publishing books.

The first clue came to me in the form of a *Forbes* article, titled "Amazon Pays $450,000 A Year To This Self-Published Writer," written about an independent author in the United Kingdom named Mark Dawson. I was impressed but skeptical. I figured maybe he was an anomaly. So, I kept reading and searching for more "realistic" examples of success.

Sell More Earn More in the United States

In May of 2017, I spoke at a writers' conference in Columbia, Missouri. Because I only presented two break-out sessions of my own, I had the opportunity to attend many other people's sessions that weekend. One of the most memorable sessions for me was Liz Schulte's break-out session. This American was one of only a handful of independent authors who were allowed to join her local traditional writers' guild. Why? Because of her *proven* sales success. She was already earning a six-figure annual royalty in her second year of self-publishing.

WHAT??!!

Now it wasn't just some seemingly "faraway fictional character" speaking to me about his success from a *Forbes* magazine article. This was a real person standing in front of me, telling me that she was doing many of the same things Mark Dawson was doing. And she was seeing similar results. Now I knew I was onto something big!

I went for a glass of wine with Liz that evening, and I soaked in all her knowledge. I also asked her to write a guest post for the PPG Publisher's Blog and she willingly obliged despite how busy she is. Thank you, Liz.

Sell More Earn More in Australia

Determined to meet even more authors like Mark and Liz, I posted a question on Quora asking authors to share their success stories with me. I received a somewhat cheeky reply from an Aussie, named Timothy Ellis, who said he wasn't sure if I would consider him a success or not because he only sells around 3,000 books per month after two years as a self-publisher.

WHAT??!!

How? Give me your success formula! Show me your stats!

Lucky for me, he obliged. Timothy Ellis willingly shared his success formula in another guest post on the PPG Publisher's Blog. Thank you, Timothy.

Sell More Earn More in Canada … and All Over the World!

Long story short, since that time, I've been a student of many more successful authors who are following similar patterns as the above three are. I've also learned all kinds of effective tools authors can use to improve their ranking on various search engines. In fact, I've studied and put into practice everything I've learned to see some success of my own over the past two years.

Here's the best part: I picked up a "real job" again about a year ago. And even with this full-time work taking up much of my time during the week, I'm still seeing some *real* progress with both my blog and my own personal book sales. So, that tells you that *you* can do the same. You don't have to quit your job and focus on writing and publishing alone in order to see success with this program. You can easily maintain both ... until you don't have to do both anymore.

Some authors begin to see significant results after only one or two years. For Joanna Penn, it took five years to transition to being a full-time writer. It took another four to earn a six-figure income. Still, it was well worth the time and effort as she now earns a *multi* six-figure income as an author and blogger. I'll tell you more about her, and why she's become one of my greatest mentors from afar, a bit later. I hope to some day meet her in person.

Everyone's journey with this will be a little bit different. But I'm going to share the kinds of activities that will get you well on your way to success—the kind of success you may not have thought was possible for an author before. Whether you're self-published or traditionally published—and whether you're selling fiction, non-fiction, or poetry—this program can benefit you if you follow it closely. That much I'm sure of.

THE AUTHOR'S MONEY TREE SEASON #1: PLANTING

Every day, people are searching for books like yours online. They perform those searches by typing various words and phrases (known as keywords) into search engines like Google and online bookstores like Amazon and Kobo. The more keywords you can associate with your book(s), and the higher your ranking grows on each of these websites, the better your chance of being found by the people searching for your topic matter.

The Power of Google in Helping You Sell Books

We'll start this book with a closer look at Google itself. This search engine powers over 75% of all Internet searches according to this April 2019 NetMarketShare report: https://netmarketshare.com/search-engine-market-share.aspx. The same report shows China's Baidu as second in line at almost 11%; so, that tells you the power of Google in helping you to sell more books. All you need now is some guidance regarding how to optimize your search engine ranking on Google, for all your major keywords, so your desired readers can easily find you.

For starters, let's call on the expert crew at Moz to explain what exactly search engine optimization (SEO) is. I found a concise description of the term in this aptly-titled article "What is SEO?" from the company's SEO Learning Centre:

> Search engine optimization (SEO) is the practice of increasing the quantity and quality of traffic to your website through organic search engine results. (MOZ, n.d.)

What constitutes *quality* traffic? It is relevant visitors to your website—people who are looking for exactly the types of books and information that you offer. What is an *organic* search engine result? It is a natural search result—one that you didn't pay for via online advertising methods such as pay-per-click (PPC) advertising. The more clickable links that direct quality traffic to a website, that show up in the top five or 10 organic search results (relative to an unlimited number of keyword searches), the more potential customers will likely visit that website. If that website happens to be your blog or your book's webpage on an ecommerce site, this will improve your readership (fan base) and help you build your name as a reputable author within your genre. And, make no mistake about it, your reputation is an important ranking factor in Google's eyes.

You see, Google was founded in September of 1998 with the sole purpose of creating a useful search experience for people to navigate through the ever-growing world wide web, so they could easily find whatever specific information they were looking for online. It was as simple as that, and Google's user base grew quickly because of it.

Unfortunately, some sneaky hackers figured out the background coding Google was using to index search results and determine which websites would show up at the top. These hackers used this knowledge to rank their own websites higher than anyone else's—whether their content was relevant to the searches being done or not. One of the techniques early hackers used is called "keyword stuffing" in which they would load their webpages full of high-ranking keywords or numbers (most of them hidden in the background) to manipulate their ranking and put them on top. The Google team caught wind of this and the first of many updates was launched—to render keyword stuffing useless and stop these types of hackers and spammers in their tracks. After all, if Google wanted to keep its user base happy, it had to keep its search results clean, relevant, and helpful.

That is the essence of every new update to this day. Google wants to keep its user base happy through these three search quality factors: expertise, authority, trust (EAT). If you maintain a consistent reputation of providing relevant and helpful content that shows your expertise, authority, and trustworthiness within your genre, you'll rank higher and higher in Google's search results over time. So, make sure you EAT regularly to keep your website ranking healthy!

Here's something else I recently read in Adam Clarke's book titled *SEO 2018: Learn Search Engine Optimization With Smart Internet Marketing Strategies* that made me smile:

> Google have been outspoken about readability as an important consideration for webmasters. Google's former head of web spam, Matt Cutts, publicly stated that poorly researched and misspelled content will rank poorly, and clarity should be your focus. And by readability, this means not just avoiding spelling mistakes, but making your content readable for the widest possible audience, with simple language and sentence structures.
>
> ...The Searchmetrics rankings report discovered sites appearing in the top 10 showed an average

> Flesch reading score of 76.00—content that is fairly easy to read for 13-15 year old students and up.
>
> ...By encouraging search results to have content readable to a wide audience, Google maximise their advertising revenues. If Google were to encourage complicated results that mostly appeal to a smaller demographic, such as post-graduates, it would lower Google's general appeal and their market share. (Clarke, 2018)

This statement makes me smile not only because it encourages editing, but also because it matches my own business philosophies that drive how I write my blog entries and books, and how I run my book publishing company as a whole. I've always maintained that when people are unable to explain their topic matter to others in layman's terms with ease, they're either hiding something or they don't fully understand it themselves. I'd rather be clear and helpful. I was glad to learn the team at Google sees it the same way. Clearly, I'm in good company in this regard.

It All Starts with a Book and a Blog

If you have published (or plan to publish) a book, you will need a website to promote it online. That's your starting point. You don't need anything fancy or expensive; a simple blog will do. If you haven't already done so, you can create one for yourself free of charge using WordPress. Just follow their user-friendly instructions along with the instructions I give you in this book.

I'm recommending WordPress here because it is the platform I use for my own blog, and I'm familiar with its plug-ins. But much of what I'm recommending here can be done without the use of WordPress plug-ins; so, if you're using a different platform, such as Blogger, that's fine. You can make that work just as well.

Why exactly do you need a blog? Think of your blog as the primary web address where you can promote *everything* related to your authorship: books (e.g., audiobooks, ebooks, paperbacks, hardcovers); upcoming book signings/speaking events; videos; podcasts; photography or sketches; questions and answers for your fans; et cetera. It's important to make your content-rich site easy for users to find and navigate because that also makes it easier for Google's search engine spiders (also sometimes referred to as web crawlers) to find and index. I'll show you exactly how to do that in chapters one and two.

Why is a Blog Better for Authors than a Regular Website?

I'll begin by clarifying that a blog *is* a type of website. Basically, anything you visit online that has its own URL (e.g., web address, domain name) is a website.

To use a familiar analogy, they're all fruit. But you can think of traditional, static websites as apples. And you can consider blogs to be oranges. One of these fruits is much juicier than the other in terms of helping you to improve your SEO and get noticed by more readers online. And your sole purpose in having any type of online presence is to do just that: attract a larger readership to your book(s).

Website vs. Blog: Apple vs. Orange

A traditional website is static in that once you create it, it just stays the same and sits there online waiting for people to view it. But a blog is dynamic. This means its content is always being updated. If you're blogging correctly, you're adding new content to your blog at least three times per week. And this is important to SEO. Search engines love new content. They eat it up! The more relevant and helpful new content you give them to share with their users, the more they'll reward you by placing you higher and higher in their ranking.

A traditional website is meant to provide basic information about you. What are your books about? Where can you be contacted? But a blog provides an expanded view of your author business as a whole. A blog is where you can share your thoughts, opinions, experiences, event calendars, and book excerpts in more meaningful ways.

Blogs allow for reader engagement in the form of the comments section at the bottom of each post. Websites don't have this ability. If you can get your readers to engage with you in this way, then you know you're having an impact with them. That's important.

Website vs. Blog: Summary

Websites are static, contain basic information, and don't allow for reader engagement. A website is limited in its ability to improve your SEO.

Blogs are dynamic, provide your readers with an expanded view, and allow reader engagement in the form of comments. Since search engines love new content, blogs are the single best way for you to improve your SEO online. But if you truly want each blog entry to be indexed by search engines like Google, then you'll have to set them up a certain way and ensure they have an optimal Flesch

Reading Ease Score (FRES). We'll discuss this in more detail in the next chapter.

Keywords are the Seeds That Will Grow Your Readership

You will want to blog about various aspects of your authorship at least three times per week, if not more. And you'll want each individual blog post to have its own focused keyword. Why? A keyword is like a seed that, when planted in fertile soil, will germinate and multiply itself repeatedly until it becomes countless more seeds of the same variety. Thus, the more seeds you plant and grow, the larger your harvest will be.

Keyword Research is Crucial to Your Success

The keywords you include within each individual blog post (and, for the independent authors reading this, within all your book descriptions) are crucial to your success. That's why keyword research is possibly the most important aspect of SEO. Because if you do all the things I recommend in this book and you obtain a high ranking for the *wrong* keywords, you won't attract that *quality* traffic you're after—those relevant visitors who are looking for your type of books. Or, worse yet, if you "put all your eggs into one basket," as it were, by using only a few overly competitive keywords on your website, you may not rank at all against the more popular and established authors' websites. It's a balancing act of adding enough different keywords to your blog entries—common and unique keywords, broad match and exact match keywords—and then monitoring them daily to "sort the wheat from the chaff," so to speak. Luckily, there are some useful online tools available to help you do just that.

How to Know Which Keywords Will Send Quality Traffic to Your Website

If you want to successfully sell books online using SEO, you need to take some time to think things through. You need to sit down and create a list of all the possible keywords that relate to the genre of books you're promoting online. Once you come up with a large enough list (e.g., 3 posts per week times 52 weeks per year equals 156 keywords), you can test all those keywords using actual search traffic data to determine which ones will be most useful for you (e.g., which ones will bring you the quality traffic you desire that has the best chance of turning into a book sale and new loyal reader for you).

Google Analytics (https://www.google.com/analytics/#?modal_active=none) is a free tool that helps you monitor your performance on search engines by tracking and reporting on your current website traffic. It can give you a pretty clear picture of where your visitors are coming from in terms of both geographic regions and sources (e.g., other websites that are redirecting this traffic to you) so you can keep track of your backlinks.

The Google AdWords Keyword Planner (https://adwords.google.com/intl/en_ca/start/#?modal_active=none) is another useful resource that you must pay to use either by running a pay-per-click (PPC) advertising campaign or by paying a monthly user fee. The keyword planner allows you to see, in real time, which of your keywords are being searched online versus which ones aren't coming up at all—so you can trash the useless ones from your list rather than adding them to your blog posts or PPC campaigns. Very useful information.

How to "Borrow" Keyword Research from Other High-Ranking Authors in Your Genre

But all that research takes time, doesn't it? Luckily, there is another free and easy resource called the SEOBook Keyword Analyzer (http://tools.seobook.com/general/keyword-density/) that will allow you to analyze the websites of other bestselling authors within your genre to determine which top keywords they're each currently using to obtain such a high ranking. When you visit the SEOBook Keyword Analyzer website, you'll see it's as simple as typing each author's web address into the box, one at a time, and then clicking on the submit button. Within seconds, a detailed list of their title page, meta keywords, and meta descriptions will appear before your eyes. You can use this data as research for your own blog's keywords.

Different Types of Keywords Bring Different Results

There's more to it than simply adding as many keywords to your campaign as you can think of that prospective readers may use to find you and your book. Different types of keywords will bring different results. For example:

- **Broad Match Keywords:** This is the default type of keyword, and it looks like this: financial planning (or this: +financial +planning). A keyword like this can trigger any number of different search results such as financial reporting, financial advisor salary, planning ahead, financial news, planning and development, and the list goes on.
- **Phrase Match Keywords:** If you put quotes around the keyword ("financial planning"), then it will

trigger search results that contain that precise phrase in them such as financial planning books, financial planning standards council, financial planning and analysis, financial planning courses, et cetera.

- **Exact Match Keywords:** If you want to trigger ads for the exact phrase *only*, then you must put brackets around it like this: [financial planning].
- **Negative Keywords:** If you ever run a pay-per-click (PPC) advertising campaign to help you sell more books, you will want to add negative keywords to that campaign to prevent yourself being charged for the clicks you don't really want. For example, maybe you've written an ebook about financial planning. If your goal is to direct people to that ebook alone, you may want to add -paperback and -magazine (with a minus sign in front of the word) to your negative keywords list. That way, you'll avoid the readers who are searching for paperbacks and magazines about financial planning.

Here's some more tried and true advice from Google Certified Professional and *SEO 2018* author Adam Clarke:

> When choosing keywords, you need a balance between keywords with a high level of accuracy, such as exact match keywords, and keywords with a larger amount of reach, such as phrase match or broad match modified keywords. (Clarke, 2018)

Balance is the key when you're planting your seeds each week. Patience will help you, too, because some of those seeds are bound to grow faster than others. That's just life.

What's the Difference Between Tags and Keywords?

Tags and keywords both help people to find information on your blog. But there are key differences between the two that are important to understand.

You may assume, as I once did, that the tags you attach to each blog post are helping your SEO on *external* search engines like Google. But those tags are simply labels that help your blog readers find information *within* your blog. For example, if you're a dietitian, you may want to assign the label "vegan protein" to all the posts you write about hemp hearts, quinoa, brown rice, et cetera. That way, all those articles will come up when readers search for vegan protein recommendations on your blog.

What Search Engines are Looking For

If you want external search engines to find each of those posts, you must assign a specific *keyword* to each post. You can do this quite easily using a plug-in like Yoast SEO WordPress to guide you on how to set up each blog post in an SEO-friendly way. How you write each post is important. It can still be effective, from an SEO standpoint, at only 300 words in length. But there are certain things you must do to ensure the search engine crawlers know exactly which keyword you want attached to that post. We'll talk about those things in chapter two.

THE AUTHOR'S MONEY TREE SEASON #2: GROWING

In chapter one, you researched and found the perfect seeds that will help you grow your readership over time. You learned how to plant them, one by one, in fertile soil. Now you'll learn how to add fertilizer and mulch to give your crop every possible chance to grow tall and strong.

10 Easy Ways to Fertilize and Insulate Your Crop

There are 10 simple things authors can do to improve your Google ranking. Do *some* of these things on a regular basis, and you'll begin to see an increase in your blog traffic which will most likely result in some extra book sales for you. Do *all* these things on a consistent basis, and the result should be a significant increase to your blog traffic, readership, *and* book sales at harvest time. The key to your success is consistency of purpose.

I mentioned earlier that Google wants to keep its user base happy through these three important search quality factors: expertise, authority, trust (EAT). You prove your expertise online by means of digital (downloadable) books and other relevant information that is published regularly and often on ecommerce sites such as Amazon and Kobo, your own blog, and other appropriate websites. Your authority is eventually proven by the number of book reviews, backlinks, plus social media followers, likes, and shares that you accumulate over time due to these publishing activities. In a search engine's eyes, if your books have more legitimate reviews than other authors' books within the same genre, your social media sites have more followers, and each of your webpages (e.g., each individual post on your blog site, each individual book on Amazon or Kobo, et cetera) have more click-throughs, then you must have more authority than the other authors have. As a result, you'll rank higher than they do. It's as simple as that, and it's all based on algorithms.

1. Publish relevant content on a consistent basis:

   Blogging is one of the best ways for you to stay engaged with your current and prospective readership; and, the more often you post something new online, the more points Google will award to your blog site thus improving its SEO. But you should know that Google is far from being the only search engine that rewards new content. Amazon and Kobo do, too. Want to *dramatically* increase your SEO over the next year? Start posting relevant and helpful content on a consistent basis that pleases *all* these search engines. That's what many of today's most successful independent authors are doing. I already mentioned a few of them in this section's introduction. I'll introduce you to a few more in the final chapter of this section. Success leaves clues … just do what they do, and you'll see.

2. Build a high number of relevant backlinks to your website:

   What is a backlink? It is a clickable hyperlink from someone else's website that directs people back to your website.

   Legitimate book reviews, guest blogging, and content syndication can be used to increase the number of relevant backlinks to your blog site. This, too, is worthy of a higher ranking in Google's eyes thus improving your SEO. It expands the reach of each seed you plant.

3. Protect and improve your SEO with REL=CANONICAL and META NOINDEX tags:

While guest blogging and content syndication are both fantastic ways to improve your website's SEO, they can also cause duplicate content issues if too much of the same copy is being reused on different sites without due care. Why? Because search engine algorithms can detect copied/reused content—and copied/reused content is a no-no in the online world, which will be discussed in more detail a bit later. For now, I'll say that this is where implementing rel=canonical and meta noindex HTML tags can come in handy:

"The rel=canonical element, often called the "canonical link", is an HTML element that helps webmasters prevent duplicate content issues. It does this by specifying the "canonical URL", the "preferred" version of a web page. Using it well improves a site's SEO." (Yoast, 2018)

The rel=canonical tag must be added to the header section of whichever webpage will be redirecting back to the URL that contains original content. The HTML coding being added to that header will look something like this: `<link rel="canonical" href="http://originalcontentlink.com/">`.

"What this does is "merge" the two pages into one

from a search engine's perspective. It's a "soft redirect", without redirecting the user. Links to both URLs now count for the single canonical version of the URL." (Yoast, 2018)

Yoast also has a WordPress plug-in that can be used to improve your blog's SEO by helping you to remove certain pages from search engine indexes altogether. Using a plug-in is an easier way for newbies to utilize HTML elements like these because they don't have to edit their website headers themselves. The plug-in does everything for them.

Which pages might you want to add meta noindex tags to? Possibly any syndicated content you posted from someone else's online publication to "beef up" your own content. You can learn more about the Yoast plug-in that can help you do this here: https://kb.yoast.com/kb/how-do-i-noindex-urls/#single.

4. Attract regular click-through traffic to your website:

It stands to reason that the more content you post, the more backlinks that redirect to your site, and the higher your SEO ranking grows, then the more traffic will find its way to your website and click on it. You want these people to stay there as long as possible. If they only click once and then leave, that's called a bounce; but, if they click on a few different pages and stay there for a while to read things over, that's called a click-through. A high bounce rate may affect your SEO negatively while you'll garner more SEO points via an increased click-through rate—all the more reason to ensure your website contains relative and enticing content people will want to stay and view.

5. Encourage more social media activity and shares (e.g., Facebook, Twitter, LinkedIn, and YouTube):

    I dedicated an entire book, titled *Successful Selling Tips for Introverted Authors*, to teaching authors how to utilize social media marketing as part of your online sales strategy. Did you know social media activity is one of the things Google rewards that can help to improve your SEO? Well, it *is*. And certain social media sites will earn you more points than others, so I've learned. For example, did you know YouTube is owned by Google? Now that you know this, you may be more inclined to start posting video content on a regular basis.

6. Make sure your website is mobile-friendly:

    On March 26, 2018, Google went live with its new Mobile-First Index which you can find more information about here: https://developers.google.com/search/mobile-sites/mobile-first-indexing. According to Google, "Mobile-first indexing means Google will predominantly use the mobile version of the content for indexing and ranking. Historically, the index primarily used the desktop version of a page's content when evaluating the relevance of a page to a user's query. Since the majority of users now access Google via a mobile device, the index will primarily use the

mobile version of a page's content going forward. We aren't creating a separate mobile-first index. We continue to use only one index." This is why I not only use WordPress for my blog but also for my company's primary website now: https://polishedpublishinggroup.com/.
WordPress sites are mobile-friendly. In fact, they look great on *all* devices.

7. Protect your website's security with SSL security certificates:

In this new world of WikiLeaks and expert hackers with the ability to break into websites and steal other people's private information, Google has become a strong advocate of website encryption. In fact, Google decided to add SSL security certificates to its list of top-ranking factors back in 2014. By purchasing such a certificate, you're providing an extra level of security to anyone who fills in an online form (e.g., a contact form, blog registration form, order form) on your website. This provides them with a direct connection to your server that no one else can eavesdrop on. Once you add an SSL security certificate to your website, you'll notice that your URL (Uniform Resource Locator, also called a web address) starts with HTTPS: rather than the standard HTTP: and has a green padlock image beside it. More and more, Google is looking for that padlock and will reward you points for having it. Luckily, WordPress sites are easily secured.

8. Include attractive images and easy-to-read fonts in your website's main content area to encourage more time on the site:

   Making your site easy for users to find and navigate also makes it easier for Google's search engine spiders to find and index; so, keep your users in mind when designing your blog site, particularly your home page. Make your blog attractive by including relevant, clickable images (perhaps your book covers with links to the ecommerce sites where they can be purchased). According to Adam Clarke, images and larger, more readable fonts can lead to a higher engagement with your site which will result in a higher click-through rate and a lower bounce rate thus boosting your Google ranking.

9. Increase Pinterest activity:

   Until I read Adam's book, I wouldn't have given that much thought to Pinterest; but, apparently, engagement with this "visual social media" website is listed as one of the top things Google is giving points for these days. If the target readership for your books is women, then set up a free Pinterest account for yourself because this site has an 80% female user base according to this article on Infront Webworks: https://www.infront.com/blog/the-infront-blog/what-is-pinterest-and-how-does-it-work. Upload images of your book covers (these uploads are known as "pins" on Pinterest) along with associated links to more information about each book on your blog. If you write on non-fiction lifestyle topics—gardening, cooking, fashion, and decorating to name only a few—then

Pinterest may be an especially great promotional tool for you. You can also share your How-To YouTube videos here to further promote your books.

10. Answer industry-related questions on your blog to encourage featured snippets inclusion:

To increase your chances of having a featured snippet of your writing included in Google searches, some of your blog posts should be formatted as detailed answers to the most commonly asked questions within your genre; and the titles of these blog posts should be formatted as the questions themselves. Believe me, your work may be well-rewarded for doing so.

What is a featured snippet? Basically, whenever you do any kind of search on Google and then click enter to bring up the results, you'll notice there are two or three listings at the very top that have the word "Ad" inside a little box to the left of their website links. And, if your search phrase was formed as a question, you may also see a large box filled with an answer to your question which is known as a featured snippet. These are both forms of Google AdWords, but one is paid for with your money while the other is paid for with your time and clever writing skills. You can think of a featured snippet as an "earned placement" for high-ranking webpages that take the time to answer common questions, relevant to their industries (or, in the case of authors, their genres), in a clear and direct way. Here's a great article explaining more about how featured snippets work: https://searchengineland.com/get-featured-snippets-site-224959.

I think this is an interesting concept in a lot of ways. First of all, it can really get one's creative juices flowing in terms of coming up with new content ideas for this week's blog posts. If you write fictional vampire novels, then you may want to write a few different blog posts such as: Why do vampires drink blood? Why do vampires sleep in coffins? Why do vampires have no reflection? Why do vampires dislike garlic? These kinds of posts will provide something a little fun and different for your regular readership, outside of your regular posts about new characters and plots in your upcoming books. Better yet, they may just earn you a featured snippet which attracts a whole new level of traffic to your blog and books.

If you write non-fiction health and fitness guides, then you may want to write a few blog entries that answer these common questions: What is the best way to lose fat fast? Will I get bigger muscles from weight lifting? How do I get a flat stomach? What is my target heart rate? Whatever questions you can think of that seem to come up repeatedly in your industry, use them as the titles of a few of your blog entries each month, then answer each question in a clear and direct Google-friendly way.

And poets? What if you answered some of these types of questions for us: What are the different types of poetry? What are the elements of a haiku? How do I write a limerick? These are just a few ideas. You get the picture. Just remember this when you're writing: keep that Searchmetrics rankings report in mind that showed an average Flesch reading score of 76.00 in the websites that ranked in the top 10 Google searches for their industries. Write for that audience for the best possible SEO results.

So, now you have a list of 10 important Google ranking factors that can help you to significantly increase the readership of your blog and books over time. To summarize this chapter, I want to share another sentence from Adam Clarke's book that I believe recaps everything we've discussed regarding the simple essence of SEO and keywords:

> Focus on improving the quality of your site, provide good mobile support, earn good quality backlinks, improve your security for users and increase the social media activity associated with your site. (Clarke, 2018)

If you consistently focus on all these things, you will enjoy a higher search engine ranking over time. And you know what a high ranking means, right? A bountiful harvest later!

SEO-Friendly Flesch Reading Ease Score (FRES)

Yesterday's advice regarding writing the most SEO-friendly blog posts was simple. Make sure your post is genuinely helpful and contains at least 500 words. Within those 500 words, your main keyword should be repeated at least 10 times. By doing that, search engines like Google should be able to easily find and index the blog entry based on that keyword.

As mentioned earlier, today's advice is a little bit different. According to *SEO 2018* author Adam Clarke and Yoast: SEO for Everyone, writing each blog post with an SEO-friendly Flesch Reading Ease Score (FRES) is crucial to your SEO success.

Why I Now Use the Free Yoast SEO WordPress Plug-In

In a nutshell, the free Yoast SEO WordPress plug-in helps me to write blog posts that Google will approve and index. That's why I use it. Because Google is the greatest link between me and my desired reader base.

As I begin writing each and every blog post, the Yoast plug-in continually gives me little notices. It lets me know whether my content is SEO-friendly in various ways. It tells me if my FRES is within the acceptable 60.0 to 70.0 readability range. If not, it will show me which sentences need to be adjusted to improve that score.

Your Blog Posts Can Be 300+ Words Long

So long as your writing style matches Google's desired FRES score, your post can be 300+ words long. Yoast also has a different way of viewing keywords. Rather than repeating your top keyword at least twice within every 100 words, Yoast wants to see it right upfront. If you include that keyword in your slug (the URL for the blog entry), at least one or more of your headings, *and* within your first paragraph, Yoast will usually give you a good SEO score. It's also great to attach the keyword to an image on your blog post, too. That way, Google will certainly understand which keyword you want the post indexed under. Make sense?

There are additional things you can do to improve your blog post's SEO. Including internal links to past blog posts and external links to other relevant information will also help. The more posts you write that Yoast awards a good readability and SEO score to, the higher up your blog will land in Google's search engine ranking under several different keywords.

10 Easy Author Blog Post Ideas

Writing regular blog posts, at least three times per week, is a great way for you to increase your online exposure and search engine ranking. These 10 author blog post ideas will inspire you to write lots!

5 Author Blog Post Ideas About You and Your Books

1. It's fairly easy to write about yourself and what inspired you to start writing at all. Make some of your 156 posts about you. Let your readers get to know you better. Maybe that will include sharing a copy of the very first story or poem you ever wrote. For example, here's my first poem in the Western Producer:

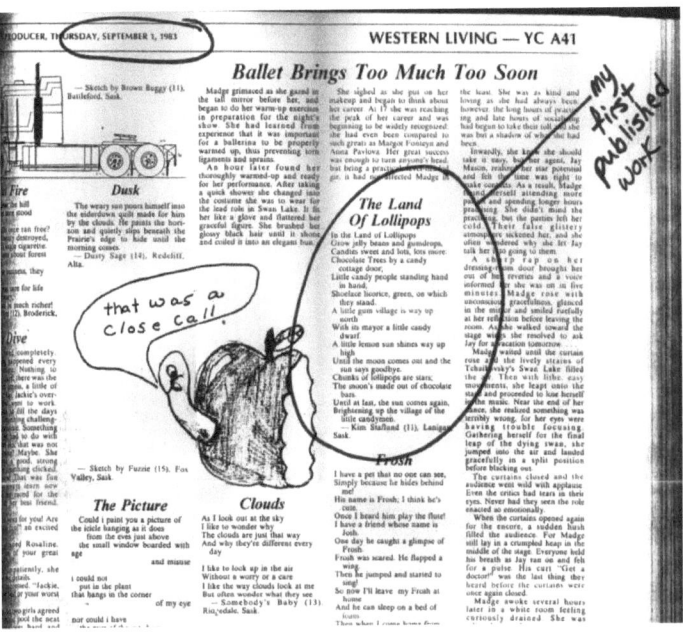

I wrote that poem when I was 11 years old; it was published a few months later, just after I turned 12. My brother found it for me in the newspaper archives years later and it put a huge smile on my face to read it once again as an adult.

2. Include excerpts from your upcoming books to create a buzz around them before they're officially published. You've probably noticed I include plenty of book excerpts in the Coming Soon to PPG! category of my blog. If you're publishing a new book at least every four to six weeks like I do, this will take care of eight or nine of your blog posts for the year.

3. What inspires you? Share the occasional inspirational quote and talk about why it speaks to your heart.

4. What is your creative process? Are you a plotter or a pantser? (https://polishedpublishinggroup.com/plotters/) Share your writing tips and strategies with your readers. Invite them to share theirs in the comments section below.

5. Do you ever attend any writer's retreats or conferences in your area? Post about your experiences, the people you've met, and the impact they've had on you and your writing.

5 Author Blog Post Ideas About Other People or Places

6. Highlight other authors within your genre whose books inspired you in some way. Review their books on your blog and include the Amazon affiliate links to those books within each blog post (see "What Does it Mean to Monetize Your Blog?" for details). If people purchase one

of their books along with one of yours, that could help your Amazon ranking through association.

7. Did you hire any illustrators, graphic designers, or other professionals to help you produce a quality book? Why not dedicate some of your posts to writing biographies about them and their important contributions? Better yet, ask them to guest post on your blog. (Remember what you read earlier about this world's "connection economy" and how to best utilize it.)

8. Read the industry news and post your opinions about hot topics on your blog. What pleases you about these current events? What displeases you? Why? Start a discussion and invite your subscribers to post their own comments below.

9. What geographic regions do your characters work or live in (for fiction or poetry), or what region are *you* currently writing in/about (for non-fiction)? Some of your posts can be geography lessons about these locations. Be sure to include pictures or videos for extra impact.

10. Search Quora for industry-related questions. Answer those questions for people on your own blog.

What Does it Mean to Monetize Your Blog?

When authors think about ways they can earn money from their writing, most think in terms of royalties from book sales. But you can also monetize your blog. The larger your blog's subscriber list grows, the more this will work to your advantage.

When you "monetize your blog," you are converting it into a source of income. Passive income. It works much the same way as book royalties do. You only have to write a book once. If people are still buying that book years after you first published it, those royalties are money earned without any additional effort on your part. Your blog posts can generate cash flow for years to come, too. It all depends on how you set up your blog.

If you are new to blogging and have only written a few posts up to now, there is one thing you can do immediately to monetize your blog. If you've been blogging for quite a while now, and you already have a pretty solid subscriber base, there are additional things you can do.

Set up an Affiliate Account Through Amazon Associates

In my opinion, the best affiliate marketing program for blogs is Amazon Associates. Why? In a word: choices. Through this program, you can sell everything and anything Amazon has to offer through your blog—not only books. You do this by creating personalized HTML links to the Amazon products of your choice through your Amazon Associates account. Then you post those links into the background coding of your website. Whenever someone visits your blog, clicks on those links, and makes a purchase through them on Amazon, you'll be paid an affiliate commission.

Set Up a Google AdSense Account

Once you've been blogging for a while and have daily traffic visiting your blog, you can apply for a Google AdSense account. What is that? Well, I mentioned pay-per-click (PPC) advertising earlier in this book. PPC is a "pay as you go" Internet advertising model people use to direct traffic to their websites. Advertisers pay only when their ads are clicked. For the campaigns that are run through Google Ads, PPC ads can show up in several places online—not only on the search engine itself. In fact, those ads can even show up on *your* blog through the Google AdSense program.

It takes a couple weeks from the time you submit your website to Google AdSense for consideration to the time they approve it. Once approved, Google will send you a unique HTML code. You can add it to any one or more pages of your website. I personally add it to the bottom of each and every one of my blog posts. That way, PPC ads appear in there that match best with the keyword and topic matter associated with each of those pages. You can do the same. Then any time someone visits your page and clicks on any of those PPC ads, you will earn a portion of Google's PPC profits from it. This is an easy way for you to earn some extra passive income from your blog.

The Value of Guest Blogging

Blogging, in general, is so important for authors. It can help you to develop and maintain an online presence which, in this day and age, is crucial to your commercial success. You can use your own and other people's blogs to share sample chapters of upcoming books as a form of advertising, and as an opportunity to receive feedback from others before publishing it. The idea of receiving feedback on your work may seem frightening at first, but constructive criticism can be so valuable to you in ways you've never thought of before. For example, many of today's top independent authors use their subscribers as "beta testers" prior to publishing—to garner useful assessments as to whether certain aspects of the writing can be improved in some way before it is released for mass public consumption. When you think of it as a form of market testing like these authors do, suddenly the feedback becomes less personal and more helpful.

Organically improving one's SEO via blogging can be a slow process—especially when you're doing it alone—because it requires a regular, consistent effort on your part to produce at least three posts per week. Most people want faster results. Luckily, there are ways you can increase the speed of this process by partnering with other people and their blogs/websites.

The value of networking with others cannot be stressed enough. Not only can it help you produce extra content for your blog, it can also create valuable backlinks to your blog from other high-ranking websites. You can learn so much from other authors and bloggers, and they can learn from you. The benefits are many as we'll discuss throughout this chapter.

When You Guest Post on Someone Else's Blog

Providing original content for someone else's blog can help you to achieve three key goals: one, it can help you to position yourself as an authority of your particular topic matter to an extended audience; two, it can bring more exposure to your own blog which may help to increase your subscriber base; and three, it can create backlinks to your blog from the webpages you are guest posting on. You'll want to partner with bloggers who post regular content that is similar to yours for an audience who will be interested in your topic matter. You'll also want to make sure the blog has a pretty strong subscriber base of its own. Better yet if the bloggers you're partnering with are active on social media, so you know they're promoting all their blog posts on a consistent basis. All these things will help to improve your chances of online success.

How do you find guest posting opportunities? Start with Google. In the search results box, type in a keyword related to your industry followed by any of the following keywords: guest posting opportunities; accepting guest posts; submit a guest post; guest post. You can also do similar searches on social media sites such as Twitter or Facebook to find guest posting opportunities for yourself there.

Before you contact any other bloggers to request a guest posting opportunity with them, you'll want to read through some of their blogs' archives and categories to get a sense of what type of topic matter is being covered. Doing so will help you to adjust your proposed content to better match what they're looking for in terms of audience (beginner, intermediate, advanced), format (some prefer point-form posts while others want longer paragraphs), graphics (if they include images with their posts then you should do the same), and word count (300 words? 500 words? more?) prior to contacting them. This will increase your chances of being accepted for inclusion on their blogs.

Your pitch letter should include a little bit of information about you as an author, what sorts of topic matter you cover in your books and your blog, and why it's such a great fit for their audience. If you have any success stories to share in terms of bestselling status of any of your books or high view/share statistics for any of your past blog posts, then share this information in your letter, too. Let other bloggers know that a partnership with you will be mutually beneficial.

Remember to keep the needs of your audience in mind ahead of your own when you're writing a guest post. What I mean by this is that the post, itself, should never be purely an advertisement for your own book or business. You can save that type of information for your author bio at the end. The post should be useful information that will help the audience in some way, whether it's to entertain them by providing an excerpt to an upcoming fictional novel or inform them with some other type of helpful guidance.

On the PPG Publisher's Blog, I allow my guest posters to include links to their latest books within their posts. I'm always looking for additional value for my subscribers (up and above the information I already provide to them) in the form of genuinely helpful tips/advice that will support them in various aspects of their book writing, publishing, sales, and marketing careers. I like to keep the flow of information open and easy for everyone involved, so there aren't any hard and fast deadlines to meet nor any specific word counts that must be met. Allowing guest posters to highlight their own books on my blog is, I believe, not only for *their* benefit (my way of thanking them for the post) but also for the benefit of my subscribers. If the subscribers are interested in picking up a book that is related to the topic matter they're enjoying, then why should they have to go searching for that book elsewhere? I want to have a link to it available right there in the content so it's easy for them to find, click, and buy. That helps everyone.

When Someone Else Guest Posts on Your Blog

The most obvious benefit to having someone else guest post relevant, original content to your blog is that it enables you to provide your subscribers with additional information without spending the time it takes to write it yourself. This is a huge enough benefit in itself. But I'll let you in on a couple of little secrets as to why I allow my guest bloggers to post links to the ecommerce sites where their books are sold: one, I can attach affiliate links to those books that allow me to earn a commission on those sales; and two, it increases the chances of people clicking on both *my* book(s) and *their* book(s) on an ecommerce site. Because it increases the chances of our books appearing on each other's ecommerce webpages under the "customers who viewed this item also viewed" and/or "frequently bought together" sections. This is one sneaky way you can make an algorithm work in your favour to increase both your sales.

What is Content Syndication?

Earlier in this chapter, we covered why regular blogging is such an important part of any author's online marketing plan. This is because it can improve the search engine optimization (SEO)—that is, the ranking and visibility—of your blog, or even the ecommerce site where your book is being sold, on top search engines such as Google and Baidu. It all depends on which webpage(s) you're promoting and redirecting traffic to within the content you're posting. When you improve the SEO for any webpage, you increase the chances of its target audience finding it.

An SEO Analogy: Retail Merchandising

When you think about it, SEO is a lot like effective merchandising in a "bricks and mortar" bookstore. It's all about positioning. The books that are strategically placed at eye level in the front aisles, or on shelving units and tables in the high-traffic areas of a store, are going to sell more than the books that are tucked away on low shelves where most people don't bother to look.

It works much the same way online. The whole point of improving the SEO of any webpage is to ensure it appears as close to the top of an online search as possible so that more people can easily see it. The higher its visibility, the better its chance of it being clicked on which translates into the better chance of a sale down the road. And that's what we're all after here, isn't it? At the end of the day, authors are blogging to promote their books with the intent of selling more copies and improving their readerships.

Here's the good news: it's somewhat easier—and much more cost effective—to improve your positioning online than it is within a traditional bookstore, particularly the major chain stores. If you want prime real estate in a major chain, allowing you to be seen by hundreds or even thousands of impulse buyers on any given day, you're going to have to pay upfront for the privilege. How much will it cost you? John B. Thompson provides details about this in his 2012 Kindle ebook titled *Merchants of Culture: The Publishing Business in the Twenty-First Century*:

> The front-of-store area that is in your field of vision is a thoroughly commodified space: most of the books you see will be there by virtue of the fact

that the publisher has paid for placement, either directly by means of a placement fee (that is, co-op advertising) or indirectly by means of extra discount. Roughly speaking, it costs around a dollar a book to put a new hardback on the front-of-store table in a major chain, and around $10,000 to put a new title on front-of-store tables in all the chain's stores for two weeks (typically the minimum period). ... Visibility does not come cheap. (Thompson, 2012)

While you can choose to pay for increased exposure online by running PPC advertising campaigns or buying banner ads on high-traffic websites, the difference here is that you don't have to. Blogging is an organic—not to mention free—way of improving your online ranking. Your only cost is your time.

Don't Get Dinged by The SEO Gods!

Now, here's the kicker: all your online articles and blog posts must be original content. Why? Because also built into these search engine algorithms is the ability to detect copied/reused content—and copied/reused content is a no-no in the online world. It is treated almost like a form of plagiarism and "penalized" by search engines in the sense that it won't be indexed by them at all; rather, it will be ignored altogether. The search engines will compare two webpages that contain the same content and choose only one—most likely the original, higher ranking page—to include in search results. The copycat webpage will fall into online oblivion, never to be seen or heard from on the search engines again.

Content Syndication to The Rescue

The obvious issue here is *time*. Where is the time to write all your books, and write original articles for other online publications, and post unique content to your own blog on a regular basis so you can organically grow (and maintain) a strong online presence? Even the simple idea of it is daunting enough itself, never mind actually doing it day in and day out. We all have busy lives, after all.

This is where content syndication comes into play as explained by Christopher Ratcliff in his article titled "What is content syndication and how do I get started?" on the Search Engine Watch website. According to Ratcliff, content syndication is great for new authors and publishers who want to expose their books and blogs to a much larger audience, but who just don't have the time or manpower to write copious amounts of new content daily.

> Content syndication is the process of pushing your blogpost, article, video or any piece of web-based content out to other third-parties who will then republish it on their own sites….
>
> Content syndication is particularly useful if you're a smaller publisher or an up-and-coming writer who wants a larger audience from a more authoritative site.
>
> By having your blog content published on The Guardian (for instance) you will be exposed to a much wider audience that isn't your own, who may then visit you on your own blog.

> The other major reason for doing this is SEO. Some of that bigger site's authority should be passed down to you. (Ratcliff, 2016)

According to Ratcliff's article, search engines are intuitive when it comes to recognizing that text links refer back to the original post; so, that is usually enough to prevent the indexing issues that stem from duplicate content. But, whenever possible, HTML coding is generally the best solution—particularly rel=canonical tags—as we talked about earlier.

Finding the Right Content Syndication Partners for You

There are many potential syndication partners available to you depending on the field you're in and the content you're writing about. It will take a bit of time and research in the beginning. What you'll be looking for are publications that: one, write for a similar audience as you write for; and two, are interested in publishing syndicated content.

Free Syndication Options (Sprint)

One of the fastest, easiest ways to syndicate your blog content is to re-publish it yourself to any free high-traffic websites that you have immediate access to—which is why I refer to these options as "sprint" options. Even better if they are channels with significant distribution networks. Three such publication channels are LinkedIn, Quora, and Amazon Author Central pages.

- **Linkedin: Best for Business-Related Books and Blogs**
  As of January 2019, eBizMBA Guide

(http://www.ebizmba.com/articles/social-networking-websites) rated LinkedIn as the 5th most popular social media site—after Facebook, YouTube, Twitter, and Instagram—with an estimated 250,000,000 unique visitors per month. That's a huge audience for business professionals of any kind, all over the world, and offers an outstanding opportunity to promote books and blogs. The Publications and LinkedIn Pulse Articles sections of this site are perfect tools for our purposes here.

Your LinkedIn profile functions as an online resume. It is here, in the Publications section of your profile, that you can feature your published book(s). Better yet, you can move sections around. By moving Publications towards the top of your profile, and marking it as a public section, it will make your book(s) appear more prominent to everyone who looks at your profile page—even those who aren't your first connections.

At the top of your profile page, you'll also notice another LinkedIn element known as Articles. This is the perfect place for you to either write unique content or share past blog posts and articles as syndicated content, as I've done here: https://www.linkedin.com/pulse/how-sell-books-linkedin-kim-staflund. You'll notice, at the top of the article, there is a place for readers to click on your profile page where they'll see your books displayed. From there, they can either send you a connection request or simply follow you on LinkedIn so that they receive notification of all your upcoming posts.

- **Quora: Great Networking Opportunities Here**

  Quora is, first and foremost, a question and answer site. It's free of charge to set up a profile on which you can promote a direct link to your blog and list any other important credentials or highlights that you wish to share. From there, you can either post questions for various other industry experts to answer for you; or, you can search for questions related to your industry that have been posted by others and provide them with well-thought-out, helpful answers. It's a great way to network with people all over the world and build up your brand's trust organically.

  But here we are again—doing more work to build our brands *organically*. It's more writing again, isn't it? Time consuming, right?

  Luckily, Quora has another feature you can utilize to post your syndicated content—which is great news because, according to a May 2017 post by the Search Engine Journal (https://www.searchenginejournal.com/what-is-quora-and-why-should-you-care/28475/), this Q&A site receives approximately 100,000,000 unique visitors per month. And it's growing in popularity all the time. What is this other feature I'm referring to? Quora allows you to create a blog on its site free of charge. Much like LinkedIn's Articles section, this is a great place for you to either write unique content or share past blog posts and articles as syndicated content as I've done here: https://kimstaflund.quora.com/Guest-Blogging-and-Content-Syndication-T-Shaped-Marketing-for-Authors. On the plus side, this site isn't limited to business-related content. Authors of poetry and fictional novels can benefit from this platform just as much as non-fiction writers can.

- **Amazon: Share Your Wordpress RSS Feed on Your Author Page**

    There's another great form of content syndication known as Really Simple Syndication (RSS) (http://rss.softwaregarden.com/aboutrss.html). If your main blog has an RSS feed like most (if not all) WordPress blogs do, then you can easily share teasers of your latest blog posts to your Amazon Author Central page as I've done here: https://www.amazon.com/Kim-Staflund/e/B0733M2PZV/. Not only is this a fantastic way to drive additional traffic to your blog via Amazon; but each time you make a change to your author page (e.g., by publishing a new book, adding a new photo, editing your author profile, posting a new blog teaser, et cetera), it acts as an update on Amazon. Frequent, relevant updates to a website are great ways to trigger Google's algorithm so your author page ranks higher in its search results over time.

As of this book's writing time, there are only five regions in the world that offer Author Central pages and you must set up each one separately from the rest: the USA, UK, Germany, France, and Japan. I've also found that only the USA page allows for links to RSS feeds, but I'm hopeful the other regions will begin to see the benefit of this and add it to their platforms over time.

LinkedIn, Quora, and Amazon are only three of the many free syndication options you can choose from. Who you work with—where you post your content to—largely depends on the audience you wish to reach. It also depends on whether you want to manually post an entire article or blog entry as shown in the LinkedIn Pulse and Quora samples, or if you prefer to have an RSS feed automatically submitted each time you post something new to your primary WordPress blog as shown in the Amazon Author Central sample.

Here is a list of some additional free content syndication tools: Tumblr, Disqus, ZergNet, Scoop.it, Hacker News, and Reddit. Reddit is one of the more popular ones that you've probably already heard of as this site covers many different topics from world news to gaming to television and the arts. There will most likely be a section on Reddit that fits well with your content—possibly even more than one.

Free Syndication Options (Marathon)

Another way to syndicate your content is to contact other bloggers and online publications who cover similar topic matter as you do. Rather than viewing them as competitors, look at them more as potential partners you can share and expand your respective audiences with. Keep in mind that content syndication of this kind is all about relationship building—and it's more of a marathon than a sprint to earn the trust of other people. You earn that trust by proving the value of your own work, acknowledging their work, and then recommending a mutually beneficial syndication partnership with them. But don't be alarmed if it takes a few tries before they go for it. Be persistent in a patient and respectful way, and you'll eventually break through.

Kevan Lee wrote a helpful post titled "How to Become a Columnist: The Ultimate Blueprint for Guest Blogging and Syndication" on the Buffer Social blog a while back that discussed how guest blogging can help lead to syndication opportunities with high-ranking online publications such as Huffington Post:

> The first step toward our syndication was guest blogging. And lots of it! Leo wrote around 150 guest posts in a nine-month period. The process was huge for spreading awareness about Buffer, building a relationship with influencers and a portfolio of quality writing, and establishing the Buffer blog as an authority on lifehacking and social media....
>
> When we chose to pitch a few sites on republishing our content, having huge hits like these gave us instant credibility. We shared our best stuff. In turn, the sites we pitched to received built-in validation that our posts would resonate with readers. (Lee, 2016)

Kevan goes on to talk about the various benefits to having your work shared by other publications. Doing so not only gives you more credibility as an authority on your topic matter, but it also opens you up to a whole new world of readers who may only stick to one publication. They would be missing out on your content if it wasn't shared with them by that publication.

For more information on how to approach content syndication opportunities of any kind, I highly recommend you read yet another article titled "Content Syndication: The Definitive, Insider's Guide" by Ritika Puri that was posted on The Buzzstream Blog a while back. One of the most helpful aspects of this post is her recommendation on how to word your pitch email to a potential new syndication partner as shown here:

> Hey {Person},
>
> I wanted to pass along a post that you might consider syndicating on your blog. It's one of our most popular posts, having generated X visits in the last Y days. Given our shared audience of social media managers, I think it could bring you a lot of additional traffic too.
>
> Feel free to use it: just make sure to attribute the original source so we don't get dinged on the SEO front. (Puri, 2015)

That's a fantastic piece of advice that is missing from so many other sources on content syndication—how to actually *write* the pitch letter! Thanks Ritika! The only thing I'll add is exactly who the person is that she's referring to in her pitch letter—it's best to start with either the features editor or the contributions editor.

How Book Publicists Can Help You Score Guest Blogging and Content Syndication Opportunities with High-Ranking Publications

On my blog, I often discuss ways authors can market and sell your books using various forms of both free and paid online advertising. Now I'm going to talk about publicity. In her ebook titled *The Power of Publicity for Your Book*, Marsha Friedman provides us with a clear distinction between the two:

> By definition, publicity is not advertising; it's coverage by the media of people, events and issues deemed to be of interest to their audiences.
>
> ...The nice thing about publicity, also referred to as "earned media," is that you don't buy it; you earn it. If you can get a journalist or talk show host interested in your story idea or topic, you might be interviewed for an article, asked to write an article for publication, or invited to be interviewed as a guest on a radio or TV show.
>
> The endorsement of traditional media, even if it's simply mentioning your name, has always been marketing gold to anyone trying to build a reputation as an author and gain visibility for their book. (Friedman, n.d.)

Some authors misunderstand the role of publicists. They hire a publicity firm assuming that organization will advertise and sell their book(s) for them, but this is incorrect. The true role of a publicist is to garner publicity for their *client*—to get that author mentioned in the media via Associated Press-style articles and press releases written about the topic(s) in his or her book, and by promoting that author as an industry expert in his or her field. The idea is to attract newspaper, radio, and television interviews that will highlight the publicist's client within the mainstream media. The by-product of this publicity is a heightened interest in the author, which should boost sales of his or her book over time much like advertising does.

Both advertising and publicity are about putting yourself in front of a larger audience as often as possible to build on (and maintain) top-of-mind awareness with your current and prospective readers; but, by contrast, advertising is essentially you talking about yourself and your book whereas publicity is the *media* talking about you and your book. Obviously, when someone else is talking about you, it has more credibility in the eyes of the public. That's the power of publicity.

There is an additional benefit to hiring a publicist to help you find guest blogging and content syndication opportunities. Publicity firms have developed long-standing relationships with all the "movers and shakers" in the media, and their staff knows exactly how to format articles to have an "Associated Press" appeal that is more likely to be picked up. They watch the news regularly, so they're aware of what is going on and how to tie you and your book topics into current events. Hiring a publicist is somewhat expensive but, in my opinion, it's worth the investment when you're working with a reputable firm.

How expensive is it? Well, it depends. There are different types of publicists out there. Some firms want a retainer, much like a law firm, and they will charge their clients for time spent researching, writing, and contacting the media as well as for telephone charges, postage fees, and any other materials they create for you (i.e., printing and copying). And then there are the firms that use a pay-for-performance business model where they charge only one lump sum fee in the beginning and guarantee a certain amount of publicity along with that lump sum fee.

Six Important Questions to Ask a Book Publicist

When researching which book publicity firm to use, I recommend asking them the following six questions for clarification.

1. Will you read my book? That sounds like an odd question to ask an organization you're hiring to help you promote yourself and your book, doesn't it? But it's an important question to ask. In my experience, many publicity firms *won't* read your book unless you insist on it. Perhaps, they don't need to. Ask them for clarification about this.
2. What are your prices? Ask for a price list of all their program options, and ask what services are included in each program.
3. What additional costs are involved in this process: do you want additional postage fees sent to you upfront and/or throughout the campaign for sending out review copies; how many physical review copies do you want mailed to you ahead of time; do you send these review copies out to low-ranking individual bloggers or to high-ranking relevant media outlets?
4. How many of the interviewers you book for me will actually go through with the interview? Do any of them cancel at the last minute, after receiving the free review copy, and then post that book on Amazon for sale? (Believe it or not, this happens. And, yes, you're right—it's unacceptable.)
5. Do you expect to include my personal phone number and email address on the press release you send out to the media? Will you share that press release publicly online via your website

and/or any other websites? How do you protect each author's privacy in this regard?
6. Will your firm find relevant and recognized media outlets who are willing to accept any guest posts I've written that link back to my own blog?

Start with those six questions and see where they take you. You'll learn a lot about the firm you're dealing with through them. Make your decision from there.

THE AUTHOR'S MONEY TREE SEASON #3: HARVESTING

Once you have planted enough seeds and grown a bountiful crop, you will have something special to harvest and share with a growing number of readers each year. It is only once you've done this that email marketing will be *truly* beneficial for you.

Engage with Your Readers in a More Personal Way

Today, most people are accessing their email messages on their smartphones just as often—if not oftener—than they do on their laptops or desktops. This is why email marketing is such an important component of mobile marketing, of *any* kind of marketing, for authors.

I was first introduced to email marketing in late 2016 when I came across a Facebook advertisement inviting me to download a free ebook titled *The Circle of Profit: How to Turn Your Passion into an Information Business* by Anik Singal. At that time, I'd been running my own digital book publishing company for seven years; and my dream, from the start, was to successfully operate this business in a virtual office environment so I could freely travel and work with anyone, anywhere in the world, at any given time. But building this online company proved to be quite a challenge. I was still having to work elsewhere, to support myself and pay my bills, because I wasn't generating enough business to earn a decent profit. I think that's why Anik's book caught my attention—because here was this pioneer of online marketing reaching out to me through the Internet, and he was willing to share his tried and true methods regarding how to turn my passion into a successful online business once and for all.

I devoured Anik's book in full over one weekend. I even read it a second time, the following week, to ensure I fully grasped every concept and recommendation he had to offer. It restored my passion and renewed my hope—along with providing actual statistics and a roadmap on how to do things right. It showed me I was already on the right track in many ways, and that I should stay the course.

> In 2012, Amazon CEO Jeff Bezos announced that Amazon's sales of digital books had surpassed their sales of physical books. Just look at how fast the Internet is growing around the world.
>
> In the last 10 years, the number of people using the Internet has grown by 600%. It's estimated that there are more than three billion people now with access to the Internet. (Singal, 2016)

According to Anik, there were only a few things I needed to tweak to get my online publishing business to take off once and for all; and, one of those things was to add email marketing into the mix. All these years, I'd been collecting email addresses through my blog and website. But I'd never utilized them in any way. I didn't know how. Anik was the first person to effectively explain the value of email marketing to me in a way that really resonated.

> Who do you trust more: a friend or a stranger? The answer is obvious: Your friend. And when your email list subscribers start seeing you more as a friend than some random person sending them emails, you'll get the best response. (Singal, 2016)

That's what email marketing is all about. It's a powerful vehicle that allows you to reach people in a more direct and personal way than other forms of online marketing can. It is your opportunity to really engage with your readers. Become their friend by letting them know a little more about you, the person, rather than just advertising your book(s) and business to them in an impersonal way. Spend some time getting to know them a little better by replying to their emailed questions with thoughtful answers.

And Anik Singal isn't the only person who swears by email marketing. While I was researching bestselling strategies for authors, I came across an online *Forbes* article by Jay McGregor titled "Amazon Pays $450,000 A Year To This Self-Published Writer." That's when I was first introduced to a UK author named Mark Dawson who was selling massive quantities of books online, and who was more than willing to openly share his success strategies during that interview. A flame lit inside my heart when I read Mark's take on email marketing because it matched perfectly with what I'd read in Anik's book earlier. It confirmed for me that I was *definitely* on the right track.

> Dawson also credits his success to his unusual attitude towards publishing. He approaches it like a business, one in which writing is just a single cog in the media machine. He engages (responding to all fan messages) with all of his fans and focusses on building a rapport to ensure their loyalty. He holds seminars to give other writers advice and guidance. And through all of these activities, he collects names and email addresses that have amounted to a 15,000 person strong mailing list. It's through this

> that he disseminates his new work. What Dawson has done is essentially build a small but loyal community that translates into near guaranteed sales. (McGregor, 2015)

The readers who know and trust you will be your most responsive buyers each time you contact them to announce a new book, product, or service of any kind. Just ask Anik Singal and Mark Dawson. But this trust must be earned over time by providing quality, valuable content to your subscribers on a consistent basis so they stay engaged with you over the long term. That's why you must plant and grow a *bountiful* crop before you try to harvest it. Always remember there are no "quick and easy" fixes in the world of online marketing. Stay focused. Be patient with the process. Be patient with yourself. But *never* give up, because your efforts will be rewarded greatly if you stay the course.

How does email marketing work? Quite simply, you want to drive increasing amounts of traffic to your blog by consistently posting new content to it that makes people want to stay engaged. You also want these people to "opt-in" to receive email notices every time you post something new there.

Not only must you obtain an official "opt-in" from every person before you can send him or her a marketing email of any kind; you must also, by law, include an "opt-out" option (also known as an unsubscribe link) at the bottom of each email you send. This is governed by the Controlling the Assault of Non-Solicited Pornography and Marketing (CAN-SPAM) act in the United States and the Canadian Anti-Spam Law (CASL) in Canada to prevent the overuse or abuse of this marketing technology. All other countries should have similar laws in place. Ensure you're properly following the regulations in your area.

What is the Difference Between Blog Subscribers versus Registered Users?

WordPress is kind of sneaky in the way it interchanges the words "registered users" (also referred to as *team members* in WordPress lingo) and "subscribers" (also referred to as *followers* in WordPress lingo) on its administrative platforms. But it's important that you never mix up these terms as per the CAN-SPAM and CASL laws mentioned earlier. Carol Manser wrote a great article about this titled "Registered Users, Subscribers & Logins: What's the Difference?" Here's what she has to say about the difference between them:

> If someone Registers on a website, they become Registered Users. Unless the site tells you that you will get some extra privilege for Registering, you will get no extra benefit from Registering.
>
> A common reason why you might want to Register on a website, is Registering on a Forum. You usually have to Register on a Forum before you are allowed to Post questions on the Forum.
>
> If someone Subscribes to a website, they consent to be put onto an Email List in exchange for whatever the website has offered to give them in exchange for their Name and Email Address details. Because of this Consent/Confirmation to receive Emails, Subscribing to a Website is not the same as Registering with a site. (Manser, 2013)

It is important to understand that when someone "registers" to your WordPress site, all they're agreeing to is the right to post comments to your blog as shown in this illustration:

Unfortunately, GoDaddy/WordPress lists these registered users as "subscribers" on your blog's admin area dashboard as shown here:

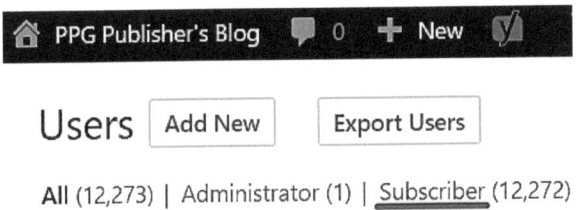

But this wording is inaccurate. Of these 12,272 people (plus me, I'm the Administrator) who are registered to be able to comment on my posts, only nine of them are actual subscribers/followers who have specifically signed up to receive updates each time I publish a new post:

Followers (9)

The other 12,263 registered users won't receive an email update when I post something new, so they're not all that useful to me at harvest time. They may never visit my blog again.

What you need are actual subscribers—*email subscribers*—who have signed up specifically to receive email updates from you. There are a couple of ways you can achieve this. First, you can replace the META widget (shown earlier) with the following SUBSCRIBER widget in your design template:

SUBSCRIBE TO THE PPG PUBLISHER'S BLOG VIA EMAIL

Enter your email address to subscribe to this blog and receive notifications of new posts by email.

| Email Address |

[Subscribe]

Anyone who signs up through that form is showing *real* interest in your blog content and books. Each time you post something new, he or she will be made aware of it with a personal email. This will dramatically improve your reader engagement.

But there is a second, possibly even better, way to collect a growing number of email subscribers who will repeatedly visit both your blog *and* your books. You will want to follow Anik Singal's lead by using a program called an autoresponder to manage all your email subscribers. MailChimp for WordPress is free for lists up to 2,000 subscribers. After that, depending on the service you use, autoresponders generally cost from $50 per month and up to maintain. It all depends on how many email addresses you are working with.

> The email addresses you collect on your opt-in page do not sit on your own computer. They actually fly into a database automatically, using a copy-and paste line of code that you've put on your page. This database of email addresses is called an autoresponder.
>
> There are many third party companies, which will manage the entire autoresponder process for you. It's incredibly easy. They give you a line of code that you simply copy and paste into your opt-in page. Instantly, the email addresses that your visitors enter are automatically placed into your autoresponder. (Singal, 2016)

Through these third parties, such as MailChimp, you can offer additional special discounts or gifts to subscribers on top of the free content already contained on your blog. For example, you can send private newsletters en masse to only these privileged fans regarding your online courses or podcasts that constitute some type of added value to them alone. Perhaps, these subscribers will be the only ones to receive discounts on tickets (or back stage passes) to the next book fair you're speaking at. I think you get the idea. For this to work well, there must be an enticing reason for them to sign up—whatever that reason may be. You choose.

Add *This* to Blogging and Watch Your Book Sales Soar Even Higher

Very early on, I stated that there are three effective ways to plant an abundance of seeds with your desired readership: productive blogging, prolific publishing, or (better yet) *both*. Ed Pilkington illustrated the value of prolific publishing rather well in his article titled "Amanda Hocking, the writer who made millions by self-publishing online" that was published in *The Guardian* online a few years back.

> In 2009 she went into overdrive. She was frantic to get her first book published by the time she was 26, the age Stephen King was first in print, and time was running out (she's now 27). So while holding down a day job caring for severely disabled people, for which she earned $18,000 a year, she went into a Red Bull-fuelled frenzy of writing at night, starting at 8pm and continuing until dawn. Once she got going, she could write a complete novel in just two or three weeks. By the start of 2010, she had amassed a total of 17 unpublished novels, all gathering digital dust on the desktop of her laptop. (Pilkington, 2012)

The article goes on to describe how, in April of 2010, she published the first of many fictional novels to a few different online platforms and saw sales of roughly nine copies per day as a result. A few weeks later, she published two more novels and saw her monthly sales grow to *hundreds* of books. A few more weeks after that, she published a fourth novel online and was amazed to see her book sales increase into the *thousands* that month! Long story short, she continued publishing every few weeks, and her sales continued to multiply accordingly. The rest is history.

Granted, Amanda's is a rather extreme success story. But the techniques she used to inadvertently become a millionaire—the top two being prolific writing and publishing—are the same techniques many others continue to use with great success to this day, whether they are writing fiction or non-fiction. Sometimes, it simply takes a few more books and a bit more time, as was the case for this non-fiction success story, Steve Scott:

> Steve talks about splitting big topics into micro-topics, which stems from his blogging background. His books are around 15,000 – 25,000 words and delve deep, rather than being the 'be all and end all' megabook which is more like the traditional publishing model.
>
> ...The tipping point into a full time income came when Steve fully committed himself to the model of Kindle publishing in Sept 2012, and wrote a book every 3 weeks. The tipping point to the big league earnings was in May 2014 when Habit Stacking took off, and having 40+ books available helped make more income from the backlist. Focus on the genre and the niche and write content within that

and build up a brand and a series. Be consistent in your writing. Make it a habit. (Penn 01, 2014)

You see? Whether you write fiction like James Patterson or non-fiction like Steve Scott, you *can* see sales success with smaller books. Throw away any pre-conceived notions you may have about what constitutes a useful book—particularly when it comes to word count. I'm here to tell you that it's more important to focus on the *quality* of your content than the *quantity* of words you've written. There is absolutely no need to add a bunch of unnecessary fluff into a book just to get it to a certain word count. Basing a book's value and saleability on word count is old-fashioned thinking. Today, you want to write for the search engines; take that 90,000-word novel you wrote and break it into a three-ebook mini-series instead. Maybe even a six-ebook series! You'll get much more bang for your buck that way.

Throughout this book, I've highlighted various authors who are seeing *significant* success in terms of the volumes of books they're selling online every single year. These four, in particular, have earned six- or seven-figure annual incomes from their ebook sales and have openly shared their stories in prominent online publications:

- Amanda Hocking was one of the first reported Amazon millionaires who utilized prolific publishing (releasing a new book online at least every six weeks, if not oftener) to self-publish her fictional books after multiple rejections by the traditional trade publishers. Of her success, Ed Pilkington wrote in *The Guardian*:

> When historians come to write about the digital transformation currently engulfing the book-publishing world, they will almost certainly refer to Amanda Hocking, writer of paranormal fiction who in the past 18 months has emerged from obscurity to bestselling status entirely under her own self-published steam. (Pilkington, 2012)

- Mark Dawson, by contrast, was first trade published. But when he saw how few copies his publisher sold of his fictional novel, he switched to self-publishing and learned how to become an *entrepreneurial* author instead. Of his six-figure success, Jay McGregor wrote in *Forbes*:

  > Dawson's recent success isn't representative of his time in publishing, however. He actually had a book published by Pan Books called 'The Art of Falling Apart' in 2000, which completely bombed. Not because it was bad - ironically it's now available on Kindle and has 32 five-star reviews out of 39 - but because few people read it or are aware of it. Mark puts the book's failure down to the publishers inability to promote his work and generate any sort of interest." (McGregor, Amazon Pays $450,000 A Year To This Self-Published Writer, 2015)

- Steve Scott is a notable non-fiction success story, proving this "rapid release" technique can work for all kinds of books—not only fictional novels. Of his success, Joanna Penn wrote on The Creative Penn blog:

> If you want a six figure income from your books, it's a good idea to model people who are already making this kind of money. Steve Scott seemed to burst onto the indie non-fiction scene in early 2014, but in fact, he has 42 books and has had an internet business since 2006. (Penn 01, 2014)

- And then there is Joanna Penn herself. I'm certain you'll fall in love with her story, as I have, if you spend enough time reading her blog posts and watching her podcast on The Creative Penn blog. Not only is Joanna personable, but she's also so willing to share her honest journey with budding authors—to show you not only what it takes, but that it *is* possible to get to where she is:

> All authors start with a blank page and no audience. You don't get from first word to multi-six-figures overnight, but it can be done if you are persistent and productive over time. Here are the significant steps on my journey from writing my first book while working at my corporate day job to multi-six-figure author entrepreneur. (Penn 02, n.d.)

These four success stories confirm what I've been writing about and teaching to aspiring and established authors alike for several years now: the most successful authors are the ones who treat book writing, publishing, sales, and marketing as their own businesses. They don't only write;

they *sell* their own books. So, although I'm sharing examples of independent authors with you here, please know this book can be equally helpful to traditionally-published authors. You can take the same steps to turbo-charge your publisher's marketing efforts; you can prevent a frontlist title from moving to the backlist by keeping it in front of your readers longer, just like these independent authors all do. The proof is in these pages.

Now, let's move onto the next section of this book and learn how you can re-harvest the same crop over and over again while growing it larger each year….

THOUGHT
The Author's Gold Rush: How to Harvest a Bountiful Crop Repeatedly

"During the gold rush, it's a good time to be in the pick and shovel business."
~Mark Twain

There is a psychology to online selling—a specific way to connect with your readers—that can ensure continued sales of your front list and backlist titles. Here's an automated system that can be repeated daily to help you earn royalties from your growing fan base again and again.

THOUGHT: THE AUTHOR'S GOLD RUSH

In section one of this book, The Author's Money Tree, you learned how to plant, grow, and harvest a bountiful readership. Section two, The Author's Gold Rush, is a simple business system that can be repeated daily. You can use it to harvest that same crop again and again with ease.

Information is Your Gold Rush

As we discussed earlier, you could be in any room chatting with your family members, friends, or business colleagues. It doesn't matter where it is or who you're with. At some point during the conversation, a question of some sort almost always arises; what's the first thing everyone does? You each pull out your smartphone, iPad, or tablet and open the web browser to search for an answer to that question. We all have instant access to timely information at our fingertips now, and we're all constantly accessing it.

People are looking for *your* information online, all over the world. Non-fiction authors and subject matter experts (SMEs) need only share that same information with a growing number of readers. Hook them by offering them something of value that makes them want more, and they'll be your fan for life. I'll show you how two authors are growing their readerships by directing new traffic to their *backlist* books.

Entertainment is Your Gold Rush

This system can work just as well for authors of fiction and poetry as it does for SMEs. Why? Because people are constantly searching for sources of entertainment, inspiration, and tribute online, too. The world is filled with voracious readers looking for a great book series to escape with in their spare time. There are just as many others looking for the perfect poem to eulogize a loved one or motivate a team.

But what good is any of this if no one can find it? Perhaps, this is your current predicament. Maybe you've already written and published a few books online that aren't getting any traction whatsoever. You're lost like a needle in a haystack. This system will ensure new readers are consistently finding all your books *and* your blog. It will help you grow your readership and subscriber base even larger, even faster—like adding lighter fluid to the fire you started in section one.

Relationships are Your Gold Rush

What you do with the readers who find you is the most important step of them all. When you personalize their experience with you and your books, they'll be your followers for life. I'll show you how one of today's top independent authors continues to harvest the same crop of fans again and again by using them as beta readers to help him improve upcoming book launches.

To build a lasting relationship with anyone, you must first build the trust between you. When they see you as an authority on the answers or entertainment they seek online, they'll begin to follow you. When they see you as a *person* they can relate to who truly cares about them as a subscriber and fan, they'll begin to view you as a trusted friend. How you think about them while you're writing for them will make a world of difference to your results.

The Digital Gold Rush

In section two of this book, we're going to cover what email marketer extraordinaire, Anik Singal, refers to as "The Digital Gold Rush" in much more detail. While my advice will be tailoured specifically to authors, there are things Anik refers to in *The Circle of Profit* that apply to all digital marketers:

> You are now going to see the power of building a business based around information. … There has never been a better time to create this kind of digital publishing business. More and more, people are turning to the Internet for information.
>
> The best part is that these people are not just looking for free information; there are millions around the world happy to pay for it.
>
> I genuinely believe that this is the modern-day California Gold Rush. I'm serious. (Singal, 2016)

It's quite simple. All you need to get started are three things you most likely already have: a computer; Internet access; the ability to write. In fact, if you've already written and published several blog entries and/or books, you're well ahead of the game. Backlist books are an asset in the online world—especially backlist *ebooks*.

The best part is that you don't have to quit your full-time job to do this. You can easily do it part-time. For Joanna

Penn, it took five years to transition into a full-time writer. It took another four to earn a six-figure income. Still, it was well worth all her time and effort as she now earns a *multi* six-figure income.

Three Feet from Gold

In Napoleon Hill's revolutionary bestseller, titled *Think and Grow Rich*, he discussed many case studies of people who had failed and succeeded throughout history. Most importantly, he discussed *why* so we can all learn from them. One of my favourites is a story about R.U. Darby and his uncle that I will share with you here.

> One of the most common causes of failure is the habit of quitting when one is overtaken by temporary defeat. Every person is guilty of this mistake at one time or another.
>
> R.U. Darby, who later became one of the most successful insurance salesmen in the country, tells the story of his uncle, who was caught by the "gold fever" in the gold-rush days, and went west to dig and grow rich. He had never heard the saying that more gold has been mined from the brains of men than has ever been taken from the earth. He staked a claim and went to work with pick and shovel. The going was hard, but his lust for gold was definite.
>
> After weeks of labor, he was rewarded by the discovery of the shining ore. He needed machinery to bring the ore to the surface. Quietly, he covered up the mine, retraced his footsteps to his home in Williamsburg, Maryland, and told his relatives and

a few neighbours of the "strike." They got together money for the needed machinery and had it shipped. The uncle and Darby went back to work the mine.

The first car of ore was mined and shipped to a smelter. The returns proved they had one of the richest mines in Colorado! A few more cars of that ore would clear the debts. Then would come the big killing in profits.

Down went the drills! Up went the hopes of Darby and Uncle! Then something happened—the vein of gold ore disappeared. They had come to the end of the rainbow, and the pot of gold was no longer there. They drilled on, desperately trying to pick up the vein again, all to no avail.

Finally, they decided to quit. They sold the machinery to a junk man for a few hundred dollars and took the train back home. Some "junk" men are dumb, but not this one! He called in a mining engineer to look at the mine and do a little calculating. The engineer advised that the project had failed because the owners were not familiar with "fault lines." His calculations showed that the vein would be found *just three feet from where the Darbys had stopped drilling*! That is exactly where it was found.

The junk man took millions of dollars in ore from the mine because he knew enough to seek expert counsel before giving up. Most of the money which went into the machinery was procured through the efforts of R.U. Darby, who was then a very young man. The money came from his relatives and neighbors, because of their faith in him. He paid back every dollar of it, although he was years in doing so.

Long afterwards, Mr. Darby recouped his loss many times over when he made the discovery that desire can be transmuted into gold. The discovery came after he went into the business of selling life insurance.

Remembering that he lost a huge fortune because he stopped three feet from gold, Darby profited by the experience in his chosen work. His simple method was to say to himself, "I stopped three feet from gold, but I will never stop because men say 'no' when I ask them to buy insurance." He owes his "stickability" to the lesson he learned from his "quitability" in the gold mining business. (Hill, 1937)

You see, there is so much more to your success than simply the **action** plan I laid out for you in section one of this book. In fact, **thought**—both yours and your readership's—will play a huge role in the outcome of your plan, as will be shown in this section about why email marketing is so effective. But, without **faith**, it's difficult to maintain one's positive thinking about any success plan. Isn't it? That's why section three will be equally important for you to read in conjunction with the first two. It is, perhaps, the greatest key to helping you stay on track until you reach your personal goal. It will help you learn Darby's "stickability" without stopping three feet from gold as he did.

YOUR SIMPLE BUSINESS SYSTEM

In the "harvest" chapter of section one, we touched briefly on the power of email marketing to help you grow your readership online. We also looked at blog subscribers versus registered users—and why you need to build your email *subscriber* list above all else. That list is as good as gold once you learn how to utilize it effectively.

> An email address (if treated properly) is worth a lot of money. It is a true business asset. A value very commonly accepted by information marketing experts is $1 per email address.
>
> That means that if you can build an email list of 10,000 subscribers, you can generate a profit of $10,000 per month - simply by properly managing that list! (Singal, 2016)

We'll look at email marketing in more detail including the psychology behind building and monetizing your subscriber base. You've already done much of the work just by writing and publishing your blog entries and books. Now all you need to do is drive more traffic to those webpages.

How to Further Build Your Readership ... in Your Sleep

Here are the three primary tools you'll be using to build your subscriber base a little larger each day: an opt-in page; a special offer of some kind; and an autoresponder. Once these are all set up properly, pretty much everything will work automatically in the background for you. This simple business system can be repeated daily, and it can literally bring you new subscribers while you sleep.

Hook Them with an Enticing Opt-In Page

If you want to build your subscriber base more quickly, you're going to need more than just a subscriber widget on the front page of your blog. You're going to want to create a specific opt-in page and promote it in strategic places online.

I recommend leaving that opt-in page off your blog's main menu. Keep it separate from everything else. Whereas other posts on your blog—perhaps even the main template of your blog—will contain links to where your books can be purchased, you aren't going to sell anything on your opt-in page. The sole purpose of this page is to entice people to give you their email address and become one of your subscribers. Period.

How will you do this? For starters, you'll want to keep the opt-in page simple but eye-catching. The main heading of the page should directly appeal to a strong pain or pleasure point for your readers. Here are some examples:

- **Fiction book series:** Love vampires? Then you'll love this!
- **Non-fiction self-help:** Too busy to make healthy, home-made meals?
- **Inspirational poetry:** Boost employee morale with this...

That's it. One line. One compelling statement that speaks to a passionate desire or problem common to your fan base. You should also add an attractive picture directly below or beside that heading for emphasis. You'll draw in more people that way.

Engage Them with a Special Offer

Underneath that heading and picture, you'll want to include one or two short sentences along with a basic Mailchimp signup form people can use to submit their names and email addresses to you. It's nice to get at least their first names so future autoresponder emails can be addressed to them in a more personalized way. But that's all the information I ever ask for to keep things comfortable—just the name, email address, and preferred subscription options.

Here are some examples of additional sentences you can include on your opt-in page:

- **Fiction book series:** Enter your email address to receive a FREE "sneak peek" into section one of the popular vampire series *The Bloody Truth About Vampires*. You'll also receive FREE updates on upcoming book launches and special offers.
- **Non-fiction self-help:** Enter your email address below to receive a FREE ebook filled with healthy meal ideas that can be prepared in less than 15 minutes. You'll also receive a FREE weekly newsletter highlighting other great recipes and special offers.
- **Inspirational poetry:** Enter your email address here to receive five FREE motivational posters for your office meeting rooms. You'll also receive one FREE inspirational quote by email each week to share with other staffers.

When people subscribe, they will receive an email shortly after clicking on the "submit" button to send you their information. (This email is already pre-set in your autoresponder as described in the next chapter.) Within that email, they'll receive the promised gift. There are different ways you can give it to them:

1. First, you can attach the ebook or printable posters as .PDF files inside the automated email. Unfortunately, this makes it a little too easy for them to share the gift(s) with others.
2. So, a second alternative is to include a private webpage link, such as this one, inside the body of that email: https://www.slideshare.net/KimStaflund/sneak-a-peek-9780986486982-publish-a-bestselling-book. This is a more secure place where they can view and/or download the file for free.
3. Or, thirdly, you can include a link directly to your blog where they can find additional links to download the gift(s) from Kobo or Amazon. Here's an example: https://blog.polishedpublishinggroup.com/free-books/. Not only is this a secure option; it can help your author ranking on these ecommerce sites as well as your blog's search engine ranking.

Manage Them with an Autoresponder

An autoresponder is a specialized tool that is used to manage all these emails as your subscriber base grows larger. Mailchimp for WordPress has a free option for lists up to 2,000 subscribers. After that, depending on the service you use, autoresponders generally cost from $30 per month and up to maintain. It all depends on how many email addresses you're working with. By the time you reach 2,000+ subscribers, if you're doing things rights, you should be earning enough additional income to more than cover that monthly fee.

You can automate so many things using an autoresponder like Mailchimp. In fact, you can use it to create more than one opt-in page for various types of subscribers—a perfect option for the authors out there who write both fiction and non-fiction, who wish to reach and grow more than one audience. Can you imagine if you had to try to keep all these email addresses straight yourself? It would be so easy to mix them up. With an autoresponder, it's all done for you in the background. The email addresses that come to you through one opt-in page are placed in a different list than the ones that come from a second opt-in page. You can set up different automated email messages and personalized gifts for each list.

Additional automation can be set up using the Mailchimp for WordPress Premium plug-in. For example, if you have a shopping cart attached to your site, and one of your subscribers visits that shopping cart but then leaves it before buying, Mailchimp will send a message to encourage him or her to complete the purchase. Just imagine how many more sales could be completed with this option.

KISS: Keep It Simple, Silly!

I don't want to overwhelm you with too much automation to begin with. It's best to ease in and keep things simple at first. For now, all you must do is this:

1. Install the free Mailchimp for WordPress plug-in to your WordPress blog site. (How to Install WordPress Plugins Tutorial:

https://www.siteground.com/tutorials/wordpress/install-plugins/.)

2. Create a Mailchimp account: https://Mailchimp.com/help/create-an-account/.
3. Log into your new Mailchimp account so you can get your unique API Key which is needed to integrate the autoresponder program with your blog. Copy and paste that API Key into the appropriate spot on the settings page of your Mailchimp for WordPress plug-in. (You'll see it when you click on the plug-in to view it.) This tells WordPress which Mailchimp site it is connected to.
4. Enable these three WordPress integrations within that plug-in: comment form, registration form, and custom. What this does is ensure that each time someone comments on your blog, subscribes to it, or supplies their email address through some other custom opt-in page, that email address will be placed into a default list within your autoresponder. You can name that list whatever you'd like to name it. For now, keep it simple and call it "blog subscribers" or something like that.
5. Now, you'll also want to let Mailchimp know which WordPress site to connect it to. You do this by going back into your Mailchimp account and clicking on "Connected Sites" within the drop-down menu under your account name. A list of various ecommerce sites, website builders, and other options will be displayed on the page for you. You'll find WordPress in the "website builders" section. Click on it there. Type your blog site's URL address into the appropriate spot and indicate that

you want all email addresses from this site connected to your "blog subscribers" list.

That's all you need to do for now. Based on all the activities we discussed in section one of this book, you should already have regular traffic visiting your blog. Now their email addresses won't only be listed for you to view in your WordPress admin area; now they'll also be placed within an autoresponder that will allow you to utilize them more effectively. We'll talk about how you can do that a bit later.

PRIMARY COMPONENTS OF AN AUTORESPONDER

There are so many things an autoresponder can do for you as you begin to grow your readership larger and larger. If you want to dive in deep—to fully understand all Mailchimp's features plus the psychology behind how and why email marketing works so well—I recommend you read Anik Singal's free ebook titled *The Circle of Profit*. A link to it is listed in the Bibliography section of this book. It's one of my online business bibles.

For our purposes here, I want to stick with the basics and keep everything as easy as possible. I'd rather have you spend your time blogging and writing books than writing daily emails or weekly newsletters. So, this book contains the essential knowledge you'll need to get started with email marketing as an author.

Email Lists/Audience

There are a few details that, by law, need to be included in all the emails you send out to subscribers. You'll fill in this information by clicking on the **Lists/Audience (depending on which version of MailChimp you're using)** menu at the top of your Mailchimp screen (the main menu) and then clicking on the email list name itself to view your contacts within that list. Within that menu, you'll see another sub-menu option called **Settings**. Here is where you'll fill in this important information.

List/Audience Name and Defaults

Under **Settings**, you're going to choose the **List/Audience name and defaults** option if you ever want to edit your list's name. For our purposes here, we'll keep it as "blog subscribers" for now; I just wanted you to see where you can change it. You'll also see some other options here that will help with your security and regulatory compliance.

For example, under **Form settings** I like to check the **Enable reCAPTCHA** box to prevent spambots from adding emails to my list. I also like to check the **Enable GDPR fields** box to ensure I can add fields to future forms that meet with the General Data Protection Regulation (GDPR) regulations related to the data protection and privacy of all individuals within the European Union (EU). This is important if you wish to reach a worldwide audience with your blog and your books.

Under the **Campaign defaults** sub-menu, I like to check all the options: **Send a final welcome email** to new subscribers; **Let users pick plain-text or HTML emails**; and **Send unsubscribe confirmations to subscribers** when they opt out of my list. To create the email, click on the **list/audience forms designer** link within that option. From there, you'll be redirected to the **Form builder** page. This is where you can edit and adjust the various automated forms (templates) that are used to create signup forms for subscribers, automatically send a thank you email to those who have already subscribed, et cetera.

> Form Builder (Final Welcome Emails)
>
> To create a personalized welcome email for new subscribers, you'll want to choose the **Final welcome email** option in the **Forms and response emails** sub-menu. You'll see how all the form fields are already populated for you, including the text for the automated email. It will simply say "Your

subscription to our list has been confirmed." But I don't just want to leave it that way. I like to personalize things right from the start, including offering free gifts within the email (as described in the last chapter), so I click inside that box and replace the one-liner with this text:

Hi friend,

First and foremost, I want to thank you for subscribing to the PPG Publisher's Blog. I hope you receive tremendous value from the information contained within.

I want you to know I plan to share so much more with you in the coming days, weeks, months ... for as long as you'll stick with me on this journey. And who am I? Why would you want to stick with me? Well, I'm someone who knows a lot about this book publishing, sales, and marketing business—someone who can help YOU to sell more books of your own.

As a bestselling author and TESOL-certified sales coach for authors with over 25 years' experience in the book publishing industry, I can teach you how to publish, advertise, sell, market, and publicize your book(s) using all the effective traditional and online tricks of the trade. Add my substantial corporate sales and advertising background into the mix, and you have a serious mentor in front of you who can help you achieve better commercial success as an author.

That's the business side of things. Now for something a bit more personal ... so you have a better idea of who you're dealing with here. I love to travel! In 2016, I achieved one of my most cherished travel goals by going on what I'll call an "Eat, Pray, Love" working holiday to Asia. This is me: **https://www.goabroad.com/interviews/kim-staflund-2016-program-participant**.

What a fantastic adventure I had! Not only did I visit Thailand, but I also got to see parts of China, Malaysia, and Singapore while I was there. All beautiful countries filled with wonderful people.

Okay, enough about me for now. In the coming days, you'll receive notifications whenever I post something new on the PPG Publisher's Blog. Occasionally, I'll let you know what I'm up to in "real time," too. Cheers to our new friendship!

Until we meet again…

All my best,
Kim

P.S. As an additional thank you for subscribing to the PPG Publisher's Blog, I hope you'll enjoy downloading and reading these free books: **https://polishedpublishinggroup.com/free-books/**. I'll also make sure you're informed whenever there are other special offers available for you to enjoy.

I want that first email new subscribers receive from me to be friendly and personalized to some degree. I want it to remind them of the value they've just signed up for, but I also want to tell them a little bit about me as a person. That starts to build our relationship right from the start. You'll see the rest of the information at the bottom of the form auto-fills with their personal information, subscription preferences, and an unsubscribe reminder in case they change their mind.

Incidentally, you can create "welcome emails" within the main **Campaigns** section of Mailchimp, too. But I just do it here. And I make sure it is sent out within one hour of the person subscribing to my blog, so everything is still fresh in his or her mind.

Form Builder (Confirmation Thank You Page)

Another form that Mailchimp creates for you is called a **Confirmation thank you page**. It defaults with a simple message that confirms and thanks new people for subscribing to your list, and it includes a **continue onto our website** button they can click on to be redirect to your blog. You can leave it this way if your goal is to increase traffic to your blog. Or, you can monetize this page in various ways. I talk about two of the most effective ways to do this in the affiliate marketing chapter later in this section of the book.

Take a look through all the **Forms and response emails** within the **Form builder** sub-menu. You may see some other places where you can personalize the automated messages going out to your subscribers.

Required Email Footer Content

Every email you send out must include more than just an unsubscribe option at the bottom. It also has to remind people why they're receiving the email in the first place, and it must include contact information and a mailing address for the list owner (which will auto-default for you). This is required by law. As such, this is the personalized message I use for my email footers: *You are receiving this email because you opted in via the PPG Publisher's Blog. We send occasional special offers as our thank you to you for doing so.*

Google Analytics on Archive and List Pages

If you use Google Analytics to track your blog traffic, as recommended in *The Author's Money Tree*, you'll be happy to know that you can also use it to track your email subscribers through Mailchimp. Simply copy and paste your Google Analytics tracking ID into this spot if you wish to do so. Google will take care of the rest for you.

Create Additional Subscriber Signup Forms

Right beside the **Settings** sub-menu, you'll notice the **Signup forms** sub-menu. This is where you can create more unique email opt-in pages and pop-up forms in addition to the basic subscriber widget that is already included with your WordPress template.

Form Builder

We already looked at two of the options within this **Form builder** sub-menu when I showed you how to personalize your **Final welcome email** and **Confirmation thank you page**. Within this option, you can also build, design, and even translate a unique **Signup form** that can be used to target specific audiences.

Just as you did with that **Final welcome email**, you can personalize the message attached to the form. Then you can share it via your Facebook or Twitter social media accounts. You can even create a special QR code that will redirect mobile customers to your signup form via the QR readers on their cell phones.

Any signup forms you create here will be assigned their own generic Mailchimp URLs (e.g., website addresses). If you prefer to use your blog's URL for all signup forms, for branding purposes, then you may prefer the next two options, instead.

Embedded Forms

When you create a new signup form using the **Embedded forms** option, you can copy and paste the auto-generated HTML code from that form into the text screen of a WordPress page on your blog. Here's what I mean by that:

> Visual Screen in WordPress
>
> When you're writing a new post or page in your WordPress blog, you'll notice there is a tab for the "visual" screen and another one for the "text" screen. The view on the visual screen will appear as it does in the top indented paragraph, with certain bits of the text **bolded**, *italicized*, and underlined. When you switch to the text screen (bottom blue indented paragraph), things appear differently. Rather than seeing actual bolded/italicized/underlined paragraph text, you'll see just plain text that has what are called HTML "tags" attached to it to. The tags are the background coding that tell the Internet what type of characteristic a particular text element has. What is HTML? **The acronym "HTML" stands for Hyper Text Markup Language** which refers to the structure (e.g., coding, markup) that is used to create a website/webpage.

Text (HTML) Screen in WordPress

When you're <u>writing a new post or page in your WordPress blog</u>, you'll notice there is a tab for the "visual" screen and another one for the "text" screen. The view on the visual screen will appear as it does in the top indented paragraph, with certain bits of the text bolded, italicized, and <u>underlined</u>. When you switch to the text screen (bottom blue indented paragraph), things appear differently. Rather than seeing actual bolded/italicized/underlined paragraph text, you'll see just plain text that has what are called HTML "tags" attached to it to. The tags are the background coding that tell the Internet what type of characteristic a particular text element has. What is HTML? The acronym "HTML" stands for Hyper Text Markup Language which refers to the structure (e.g., coding, markup) that is used to create a website/webpage.

You're going to cut and paste that code for your newly-created embedded signup form into the text screen of the whichever WordPress page you've decided to use as a signup page. Once you've done that, and you go back to the visual screen view, you'll see the actual form there.

Here's an example of how an embedded form might look on a blog post: https://polishedpublishinggroup.com/the-authors-holy-trinity-of-profit/. I created this particular opt-in page using a blog *post* as opposed to a new blog *page* because I wanted it to show up on my Amazon Author Central page through my blog's RSS feed. Doing so helps with pre-promotion of the book on one of the top ecommerce sites where my books are sold.

For details on how to set up this kind of syndicated content feed on Amazon, please refer back to The Author's Money Tree section of this book. In the meantime, you may also want to pick up a copy of my recent *HTML Coding for Beginners* mini ebook from either Kobo, Amazon, or E-Sentral for more help understanding HTML.

Subscriber Pop-ups

You can also use Mailchimp to create special subscriber pop-ups for your blog. No need to copy and paste any code from here into your blog. Simply create the pop-up, then click on "publish" and let Mailchimp do the rest. Since Mailchimp and your WordPress site are already linked together, it will automatically attach the pop-up to your blog for you.

Your pop-up message can say something as simple as "Subscribe here to be first in line for new book release news! You'll also receive first dibs on FREE book downloads and coupon codes for other special offers as they arise." Remember, you want to offer people something of value in exchange for their email address here, just as you would do on any other opt-in page.

Create Email Campaigns to Engage with Your Readers

If you're following the instructions from section one of this book, then you're already blogging and publishing in very specific ways regularly. That's increasing your author ranking *and* search engine ranking which is bringing you more and more traffic each day. That traffic is building your readership and blog subscriber base each day, too.

To ensure most (if not all) of your subscribers are buying your books, it's important to engage with them in a personalized—but highly efficient—manner just like the authors I mentioned earlier all do. This can be done via Mailchimp's main menu option titled **Campaigns**. There are a variety of campaign options for you to choose from here.

Broadcast Emails (A Monthly Newsletter)

Here is where you can create a monthly newsletter that highlights this month's favourite blog posts/podcasts/videos, upcoming book launches, any other special author events you'll be attending, et cetera. It's also a great place to offer discounts on select books—to let your subscribers know when and where these books will go on sale or be offered free of charge for them only, for a limited time only. A newsletter is intended to broadcast timely, current events to your subscribers; it's meant to remind them that there's a *real* person behind these emails who truly values them as blog subscribers and fans of your books.

When you first set up your Mailchimp account, you'll be prompted to design your first email campaign within the main **Campaigns** menu by clicking on the **Create Campaign** button on the top of your screen. You'll find a great newsletter template in the default **Regular** section of the **Email** sub-menu.

First, you're going to want to give this campaign a name. (I call mine "PPG Publisher's Blog: Monthly Newsletter" to keep it clear and simple.) Once you've named your campaign and clicked on the **Begin** button, the next screen will appear where you can create your newsletter by adding your "blog subscribers" list to the recipients list. You should also personalize the "To" field with *|FNAME|* as opposed to just leaving it generic. These little personal touches make a difference to your subscribers, trust me.

The bottom **Content** portion of this form is where you'll choose whatever template you want to create your newsletter with by clicking on **Design Email**. There are several featured templates to choose from. I prefer the **Tell a story** format for newsletters; it's up to you which template you use.

Mailchimp won't let you send your email to anyone until you've replaced all the placeholder content with your own personalized content. This is a great built-in safeguard. Once you're done creating the newsletter, you can schedule when you're going to send it—whether that's right now, later today, or on another day in the near future. (If you read *The Circle of Profit*, as recommended, you'll learn all kinds of tips and statistics behind which days of the week are best for sending out emails and why.)

Mailchimp will take care of the rest and even let you know how many of your subscribers opened the email, how many of the emails bounced due to being sent to invalid addresses, et cetera. You can use this data to clean up your list, from time to time, to ensure it only contains valid email addresses with interested readers in it. Cleaning up will become more important the larger your list grows because your monthly Mailchimp subscription price is based on how many subscribers/emails the autoresponder is managing for you.

Automated Emails (Share Your Blog Posts)

Since your WordPress blog has an RSS feed, you can easily share teasers of your latest blog posts with your email subscribers in the same way you're sharing them as syndicated content on your Amazon Author Central page. You do this by setting up a new email campaign.

First, you'll need your blog's RSS feed link. On WordPress, you'll find a link to it in your META widget titled **Entries RSS** as shown here:

META

Register

Log in

~~Entries RSS~~ (circled)

Comments RSS

WordPress.org

You can click on that link to be redirected to the feed. Or, you can simply type "feed/" after your blog's main URL in order to bring it up. For example, my blog's RSS feed is located here: https://polishedpublishinggroup.com/feed/.

Now, to set things up so that your new blog posts are automatically sent out to your email subscribers, you'll want to go back to the main **Campaign** menu and click on the **Create Campaign** button again. Click on the **Email** sub-menu again. But, this time, you'll want to choose the **Automated** option at the top, second from the left. Here is where you'll find a box that says **Share blog updates** on it. Click on that box.

I like to name this email campaign "PPG Publisher's Blog Updates and Special Offers." You can call yours whatever you want to call it. That name is there simply to remind you what the campaign has been created for. Once you name it and choose your list, you'll be redirected to the next screen where you can copy and paste your blog's RSS feed into the appropriate spot.

If you think your subscribers will be okay with receiving an email every time you write a new post, you can keep the default options as they are. Anik Singal believes the more emails the better, but I think there's such a thing as overkill. Because I only publish up to three blog posts per week, I leave all the default options as they are so that my subscribers are getting each new post in real time; and I send a newsletter once a month to recap that month's highlights for them. I also always personalize the "To" field with ***|FNAME|*** as opposed to just leaving it generic.

Once you click through and choose all your options, you'll be asked to pick a template just as you did for your newsletter. I prefer my blog updates to look different than my newsletter, so I choose a basic text message for these. Whatever template you use, make sure you include these RSS content blocks within the template: **RSS Header** and **RSS Items**. If you leave these out, the blog entries from your RSS feed won't show up in the email. The rest of your content blocks and overall design is up to you.

It's always best to preview and test each email campaign you create through Mailchimp before you save the final version. This will allow *you* to see exactly what your subscribers will see once you launch the campaign. I do this for all of mine. I preview them on my screen; I also send myself an email so I can see how it will look to others. Only when I'm satisfied with these test results do I approve anything for launch.

PPC Ad Campaigns (Facebook/Instagram and Google)

Mailchimp also helps you to create pay-per-click (PPC) advertising campaigns on Facebook/Instagram and Google. What is PPC advertising? PPC is an Internet advertising model used to direct traffic to various websites (also known as landing pages) in which advertisers pay as they go, only when their ads are clicked. It is defined simply as "the amount spent to get prospective buyers to click on an advertisement."

The cost of a PPC campaign depends on a few different factors:

1. Where is it being run (i.e., Google or Facebook)?
2. What region is it being targeted to (i.e., one city, province, or state, an entire country, an entire continent)?
3. How long will the campaign run for (i.e., for a specified amount of time, or until a specified advertising budget has been used up)?

This is a great tool to help you promote your blog and/or books in more strategic places online. When you start a PPC campaign, you agree to pay X dollars per each click on your ads that are redirected to a specified landing page (e.g., opt-in page), your blog's main page, or the ecommerce webpage where your latest book is being sold (hence the term "pay-per-click"). Where Google campaigns are designed to target specific keywords that users might type into the search engine, Facebook campaigns are designed to target a specific demographic such as "female users, age 20–40" or "all users" who have expressed an interest in "book publishing," as two examples.

To create a PPC campaign through Mailchimp, click on the **Ad** sub-menu option under **Campaigns**, then choose either the **Facebook/Instagram ad** option or the **Google remarketing ad** option. Name your campaign whatever you'd like to name it. Perhaps you can call it either "FBI for *Your Book's Title*" or "Google for *Your Book's Title*" to keep things simple.

Facebook PPC Ads

On the next page, you can choose which channel you'd like to run your PPC ads in: Facebook, Instagram, or both. You do this by first linking your social media accounts to your Mailchimp account which is as simple as clicking on each option and then logging into them through Mailchimp.

Mailchimp keeps your next four choices fairly simple and straightforward:
- if you choose "new people" then you can indicate which geographic region, gender, age, and interests you wish to target that are similar to your existing contacts;
- if you choose "contacts" then you can target either an existing Mailchimp list or the list of people who have liked your Facebook page;

- if you choose "custom audience" then you can again indicate which geographic region, gender, age, and interests you wish to target to find a new audience;

- or, last but not least, if you have a paid Mailchimp account, you can also choose to target any of the people who have visited your website, but haven't subscribed to it yet, using Facebook pixels. (About Facebook Pixel: https://www.facebook.com/business/help/742478679120153.)

After that, you can choose your daily, weekly, or monthly PPC budget. Then design your ad.

Google PPC Ads

With Google ads, your goal is to bring more traffic to your blog itself as opposed to your social media sites. If your WordPress account isn't already properly connected to your Mailchimp account, you'll be given a bit of HTML code that you'll need to copy and paste into the <head> section of your blog's theme. You will find that <head> section in your WordPress admin menu item titled **Appearance** and the sub-menu item titled **Theme Editor**. From there, you'll see another menu on the righthand side of the screen titled **Theme Files**. You'll want to scroll down that menu until you reach **Theme Header (header.php)** and click on that. The HTML coding for your theme's header section will now appear in the centre of your screen. All you must do is copy and paste the HTML code from Mailchimp somewhere in between <head> and </head> within that main theme HTML code. Then click on the **Update File** button at the bottom to save it before logging back out of WordPress. (Here's a great Mailchimp article with clear step-by-step instructions on how to do this in case you need more help with it: https://Mailchimp.com/help/about-connected-sites/.)

After that, you can choose your weekly PPC budget. Then design five different PPC ad options for your campaign.

For more information about how PPC advertising works on various online platforms, including LinkedIn, you may want to pick up a copy of my recent *Pay-per-click (PPC) Advertising* mini ebook from either Kobo, Amazon, or E-Sentral. It also goes into more detail about how Google Adsense can be used to monetize your blog.

Landing Page

Mailchimp's **Landing page** option contains the following templates to help you design attractive opt-in pages with specific goals in mind:

- Accept Payments
- Generate Leads
- Grow Your List
- Promote Products

Much like the sign-up forms you create within the **Form builder** sub-menu, any landing pages you create here will be assigned their own generic Mailchimp URLs (e.g., website addresses). If you prefer to use your blog's URL for all signup forms, for branding purposes, then just use the **Embedded forms** option within the **Signup forms** sub-menu.

SUPERSIZE ME!

In section one of this book, I talked about how UK author, Mark Dawson, used email marketing (among other things) to earn $450,000 in one year from his readership. In Anik Singal's book, *The Circle of Profit*, he discusses how he was able to scale his own "information product" business to $3,000,000 using similar strategies.

> The simplicity of this Circle is a gift. It is this very gift that allows you to focus on your life while letting the business run itself. You can use the following system to make $100,000 a year, $10 million a year, or even $100 million a year. I have no doubt anymore about the scalability of this system. (Singal, 2016)

What Anik refers to as an information product, we authors simply call a book or a blog. Other than that, the strategies used are pretty much the same:

- create an enticing opt-in page and drive traffic to it using the strategies discussed in sections one and two of this book;
- encourage people to become email subscribers to your blog via that opt-in page by offering gifts or special offers of some kind;
- further engage with your subscribers through regular blog posts and a monthly newsletter that offer deals on books and additional items of value (some of which will be discussed in this chapter);
- personalize their experience to keep them interested;

- make sure they're aware of each new book you release and encourage them to buy;
- lather, rinse, repeat.

That's how you earn a profit at this over time—by growing your readership bit by bit every single day. You set everything up with an auto-responder and let it run in the background while you continue doing what you love best—writing! How perfect is that? I swear this whole online business world was built just for us writers. (Even Anik has a section in his book devoted to teaching other online marketers where to hire writers to help them create their information products. We writers are precious commodities, my friend! Don't ever let anyone else try to tell you differently.)

Now, there are some additional things you can do to scale your business even larger than you may have originally expected. Anik refers to this as building a $1,000,000 sales funnel:

> A funnel is a group of products that are strategically sold, one by one, to existing customers.
>
> For example, let's say you go to McDonald's and order a Big Mac. The cashier behind the register asks, "Do you want fries with that?" Then he asks if you'd like a soda, too.
>
> You were just the target of a small sales funnel: After you agree to become a customer by asking for a Big Mac, the company positions other beneficial and complementary offers in front of you.
>
> By adding French fries and a soda to your order (simply by asking you), McDonald's just doubled

the size of your order. Multiply that by millions of daily Big Mac eaters, and just imagine what that funnel does to their revenue. (Singal, 2016)

This chapter is all about how you can design an automated sales funnel to sell more frontlist *and* backlist titles to your readership. You can use it to promote additional books in a series or other complementary products and services (e.g., online courses, a podcast, et cetera). You can even use this strategy to get loyal readers to sign up as affiliate marketers who sell your books *for* you.

Would You Like Fries with That?

The very first automated email your subscribers will receive from you, one hour after subscribing to your list, is the **Final welcome email** mentioned earlier. There's a good reason why I want you to personalize that email to include a sentence that reads something like this: "I'll also make sure you're informed whenever there are other special offers available for you to enjoy." It's because this sets up their expectation of receiving additional deals—so they're anticipating future emails from you. That way, they'll be more likely to click on those emails and open them.

Vary Your Automated Blog Post Notifications

It's important to vary the information contained in each blog post you write so your subscribers stay interested in the blog post notifications they receive from you by email. In section one of this book, I gave you 10 easy blog post ideas to choose from.

- Some are different types of educational posts that teach your subscribers new concepts or skills, or

- that answer questions they may have recently emailed to you.
- Others are promotional posts that sell your new (frontlist) books/products/services and contain links to where each of these items can be purchased.
- And then there are the "insider" entertainment posts that share personal information about you and your life, your opinions on hot topics, quotes that inspire you, et cetera.

When you get personal with your subscribers in this way, you'll get the best response from them in return. Why? Because they'll view you as so much more than a distant author of books they enjoy reading; they'll see you as a real person, maybe even a friend.

A new blog post category I incorporated this past year is my Blogging Progress Reports. I was inspired by Joanna Penn to share all my "micro wins" along the way, just as she did, so you can see my *true* journey to success as an author. I hope doing so makes it all feel more possible for you on those days when you're questioning everything. That's what Joanna did for *me* when she very openly shared her own roadmap to a multi-six-figure income—the "macro win" that came later—on her blog.

But Joanna does so much more than just blogging and publishing books. She is where she is because she has created a sales funnel similar to what Anik Singal recommends. She's learned how to "add fries and a soda" to each of her orders with a podcast, YouTube video channel, online courses, et cetera. Visit her website, and you'll see exactly what I mean: https://www.thecreativepenn.com/.

Set Up Five Automated Backlist Emails

An easy way to sell your older (backlist) books/products/services is to automate five more emails that will be sent out to subscribers, roughly one week apart, following the **Final welcome email**. Try to set these up to go out on different days than your blog post notifications and monthly newsletter broadcast so you don't have any overlap.

In these five emails, you may want to:

- offer specials for the first books of past series;
- redirect people to important one-off backlist titles (e.g., I promote an important book I wrote a year or two ago, that is still relevant now, that answers people's most common book printing questions);
- and/or promote relevant online courses (e.g., I'm set up as an affiliate marketer with Udemy.com where I sell both my own and others' online courses about writing and publishing here: https://polishedpublishinggroup.com/sales-coaching-for-authors/).

How you design these emails will be critical since it's a little trickier to move a backlist title than a new one. You'll want to incorporate the five "psychological hacks" mentioned a bit later in this chapter, in The Psychology of Email Marketing section. Doing so will improve your success rate.

Invite Subscribers to Become Your Affiliate Marketers

Another effective way to engage your fan base is to offer them incentives to help you with the promotion of your books. You can offer a free copy of one or two of your ebooks to those who are willing to share a book launch announcement with their own social media networks. Better yet, you can show your fans how to register as affiliates with the ecommerce merchant(s) you're selling your books through. Once their affiliate profiles are approved by a merchant, they can then download customized affiliate links to your books that will track directly to their profiles, and they can share *those* links on their blogs and social media websites, or even via email at launch time. It's like having a 100% commission sales force working for you, no upfront investment necessary, as described in this post titled "Affiliate Marketing 101: Part I" on the Acceleration Partners® blog:

> WHAT IS AFFILIATE MARKETING?
>
> Essentially affiliate marketing involves a merchant paying a commission to other online entities, known as affiliates, for referring new business to the merchant's website. Affiliate marketing is performance-based, which means affiliates only get paid when their promotional efforts actually result in a transaction. (AccelerationPartners®, 2014)

As the author, you don't have to track or pay for anything at all. These transactions are between the affiliates and the online merchants they registered with. At the end of the day, you'll still get paid whatever royalty percentage you would normally be paid for the sale of your books on each merchant's website, and the affiliate commissions will be taken care of for you in the background. It's a win-win-win scenario for you, the affiliate marketer, and the retailer.

Amazon Associates

Amazon's affiliate program is called Amazon Associates and it can be found here: https://affiliate-program.amazon.com/home. Through this program, people can sell everything and anything Amazon has to offer—not only books. The only issue I have with their program is that affiliates must register, over and over again, for each separate website (e.g., Amazon.com, Amazon.ca, Amazon.co.uk, et cetera) in order to sell things to people around the world. That said, they've recently implemented a new strategy they call OneLink (https://affiliate-program.amazon.com/onelink/) that allows you to combine all those sites together as one after you've registered on them all. Believe me, this is a blessing.

Before OneLink came along, if you included an Amazon.com affiliate link on your blog for people to purchase from, it would only work for the American buyers who made a purchase through that link. It wouldn't register as an affiliate sale for any of your other buyers outside the United States because, when *they* clicked on the link to buy the item, they would be redirected to the Amazon site in their own regions. To earn a commission from all the Amazon markets around the world, affiliates had to display separate affiliate links for every single market—and there are *several* so that was a royal pain in the butt. Luckily, OneLink has resolved that issue. Now affiliates only need to add one main Amazon.com link to their sites and the other international sales will be taken care of through it. This makes me a very happy affiliate marketer!

Kobo Affiliate Program

The Kobo Affiliate Program (found here: https://kobowritinglife.zendesk.com/hc/en-us/articles/115008616207-Kobo-Affiliate-Program) works much the same way. Although it appears their program is currently only available in six regions (e.g., Canada, US, UK, Australia, France, Germany) compared to Amazon's twelve regions (e.g., US, UK, Germany, France, Japan, Canada, China, Italy, Spain, India, Brazil, Mexico), this is a fast-growing ecommerce retailer that is quickly catching up to its competition.

You can also become an affiliate marketer for other Amazon products that complement your book series. And you can list your own affiliate links to these products within the **Confirmation thank you page** that automatically goes out to new subscribers rather than using the default option of redirecting them back to your website. Here are a couple of examples:

- **Fiction book series about vampires:** Redirect them to an affiliate link like this one (https://amzn.to/2FinsDa) where they can buy vampire teeth simply by adding the link into the content portion of the default email.

- **Non-fiction self-help recipes:** Here's a cool Fruit Infusion Natural Fruit Flavor Pitcher that might complement your healthy recipe series: https://amzn.to/2OoQPI5. You can use this link as your **Confirmation thank you page** URL rather than the default signup form URL.
- **Inspirational poetry to boost employee morale:** Perhaps this Success Gift Pen with LED Light and Stylus Tip would be a nice complement to your inspirational poetry: https://amzn.to/2FmUTVj. Again, it's your choice whether you add the link into the email or use it in place of the default **Confirmation thank you page** URL.

Setting up an affiliate profile—and encouraging your followers to do the same—is an easy way to earn passive income. You need only set it up once and then automate it by including it as part your **Confirmation thank you page**.

Another thing you can do to monetize your **Confirmation thank you page** is to redirect new subscribers to your Amazon Author Central page (such as this one: https://www.amazon.com/Kim-Staflund/e/B0733M2PZV). This way, they're seeing all your books together and can buy them direct rather than buying someone else's product through an affiliate link.

Invite Subscribers to Become Your BETA Readers

In the traditional publishing world, your edited book is sent to a professional proofreader for a final once-over before publication. In the digital world, you can complete that final proofread yourself; or, you can do what some of today's entrepreneurial authors are doing to ensure that polished result we're all after. Authors such as Mark

Dawson and Don Massenzio are combining proofreading together with a form of market research in order to sell more books: they're using their top fans as BETA readers. In his blog entry titled "The Importance of an Editor and Beta Readers for Independent Authors," Don Massenzio explains how using your own loyal readers as focus groups can improve the quality and enjoyability of your books for everyone:

> Beta readers are early previewers of your book that read through it after the editing process is complete. They look for story element inconsistencies and other elements of your book from the perspective as [sic] a fan and a reader. It's a good idea to pick a couple of readers that are big fans of your writing, but are not afraid to give suggestions. This process is like having a focus group or preview audience for your product that gives their opinion to you on a small scale before you release it to the relentless general public. Beta readers will spot things in your book that you and your editor missed such as inconsistencies in character traits, likability of your characters, and other intangibles. This is especially importance [sic] if your characters span more than one book in a series. You don't want to publish a book in a series that has continuity issues with previous books. (Massenzio, 2015)

I've mentioned Mark Dawson throughout this book because he is a highly successful and business savvy author that was mentioned in *Forbes* as earning $450,000 per year selling his books online. Mark not only writes and publishes several books per year, but he also uses beta readers to improve each books' saleability come publication time. So, this technique is definitely worth consideration. It is a new take on proofreading that may well be the wave of the future.

> One of the practices that many Indie authors have implemented is an advance or beta team of readers who serve the author in a few very important ways in exchange for a free, advanced copy of the book. #1 - These readers help tighten up plot holes, errors, and oversights through feedback as they read the book. #2 - They provide reviews on Amazon and other retailers once they [sic] book is live on their platforms. #3 - They also can be a great source of encouragement and affirmation for the author. Mark's beta reader team was fairly large (over 700 people) and they were very active in this most recent launch. (Dawson, 2016)

It's up to you: hire a professional proofreader; proofread it yourself; or, use BETA readers to proofread your books. At the end of the day, the path you choose will depend on your budget and personal preference. But I *do* recommend a final proofread of some kind, however you get it done. It will polish your book even further than a copy edit does which should positively impact your sales in the long run.

The Psychology of Email Marketing

I recently came across an article by Bernard Meyer titled "5 Email Marketing Psychology Hacks to Boost Engagement & Sales." It's a great read about various scientific studies that were done to better understand people's behaviours and how each can be applied to help you design more effective emails.

> Implementing psychological hooks in your email marketing campaigns can not just boost sales, but can also help you skyrocket your engagement and brand loyalty rates.
>
> After all, understanding psychology allows you to guide your subscribers and customers to take the desired action. This helps you get better sales, but it also allows your customers to quickly see the value you're offering. (Meyer, 2018)

The five studies refer to:

1. price anchoring (displaying a significantly more expensive book beside your own on the same topic can make yours look more attractive);
2. the paradox of choice (segmenting your email campaigns, rather than sending "everything to everyone," will improve engagement by preventing the state of "analysis paralysis" that is created by too much choice);
3. the fear of missing out (creating scarcity or urgency with "limited time offers" can entice people to buy now);
4. the foot in the door technique (getting subscribers to agree to a smaller request, at first, will make them more willing to agree to larger/pricier requests later);
5. and reciprocity (taps into some people's need to give back to you after you've given them something for free).

I highly recommend you read the article (which is hyperlinked in the Bibliography section at the back of this book). Read the individual studies to learn more about how and why these techniques work, then keep them in mind as you design each of your emails.

Scale It Larger by Reinvesting

As soon as you begin to earn profits from this business system, you really should get into the habit of saving 10% of it into a "rainy day" fund and reinvesting at least another 10% of it back into your business. You can use some of this profit toward more PPC advertising to grow your email lists larger in your sleep. As you earn significantly more, you can also use it toward hiring a publicist to help you syndicate more of your content. That's when you'll begin to see a more rapid growth rate and realize the true scalability of a digital publishing business.

But things will take some time in the beginning, hence the "rainy day" fund. If you expect some struggles right from the start, you'll handle it all much better and have that "stickability" R.U. Darby had to learn about the hard way.

> Before success comes to most people, they are sure to meet with much temporary defeat, and perhaps some failure. When faced with defeat the easiest and most logical thing to do is to *quit*. That is exactly what the majority of people do.
>
> More than 500 of the most successful people America has ever known told the author their greatest success came just one step beyond the point at which defeat had overtaken them.

> Failure is a trickster with a keen sense of irony and cunning. It takes great delight in tripping one up when success is almost within reach....
>
> [R.U. Darby] recalled, too, his mistake in having stopped only three feet from gold. "But," he said, "that experience was a blessing in disguise. It taught me to keep on keeping on, no matter how hard the going may be, a lesson I needed to learn before I could succeed at anything." (Hill, 1937)

Even if you run into any "fault lines" as R.U. Darby and his uncle did, never give up. Seek expert advice from the many successful people mentioned throughout this book. And remember my own struggles that I shared with you at the very beginning of The Author's Money Tree section—struggles I will explain in more detail in the The Author's Magic Key section coming next. I'm sharing them to let you know that we've all been there, and we're a community of people willing to help you when you need it.

This system *can* work for you as it has worked for so many others before you. I'm absolutely convinced that it can work for non-fiction, fiction, and even poetry authors. This digital publishing age is the author's gold rush, and I hope you strike it rich! To help you do so, let's take a look at the next necessary ingredient: faith.

FAITH

The Author's Magic Key: How to Stay on Track and Keep the Faith

"Books are uniquely portable magic."
~Stephen King

You're going to experience self-doubt along the way. You may even run into some naysayers who try to tell you that your books are unsaleable. Here are words of wisdom and inspiration, from those who have succeeded before you, to help you through those times.

FAITH: THE AUTHOR'S MAGIC KEY

Just as it takes three full seasons to reap the *true* rewards of The Author's Money Tree, there are three necessary components to achieving your goals. Action. Thought. Faith. The final section in this book focuses on helping you develop a strong faith in yourself and your craft.

The Magic Key to Faith

To see this plan through to fruition, you'll need to have complete confidence and trust in what you're doing. You'll need to hold true to your goals even on those days when your progress seems slower than you'd like.

One of the best ways to develop faith is to read the stories of others who have succeeded before you. This book is filled with many of the sources I often turn to for inspiration. Some of these people are authors. Others are business owners, actors, or athletes. They all have one thing in common: a strong, unwavering faith in their own abilities that was developed over time.

The Magic Key to Focus

They also have a laser focus on reaching their desired goals, whatever those goals may be. They visualize their desired result daily before taking action. And they train their brains with the use of affirmations, as recommended by Napoleon Hill:

> The method by which one develops *faith*, where it does not already exist, is extremely difficult to describe. Almost as difficult, in fact, as it would be to describe the color of red to a blind man. Faith is a state of mind that you may develop at will ... Making repeated affirmations to your subconscious mind is the only known method of developing the emotion of faith voluntarily. (Hill, 1937)

This book is filled with many teachers who can help you achieve your goals under any circumstance. Even if you don't have any "cheerleaders" around you.

The Magic Key to Endurance

Let's face it, some days are easier than others when it comes to sticking to any goal. We all have our moments of doubt. Sometimes, it would be easier to quit.

It doesn't matter who you are, you're going to have setbacks. It's at those times when you'll need a little boost to help you get back on track. In this book, I've included the inspirational stories of several people who have succeeded before you. But I don't want you to see their successes alone; in fact, I want you to see their failures. Because I want you to see how they got back up again—how they endured through difficult times—so you know you can do it, too.

Whenever you're struggling along your journey as an author, I hope you'll pick up this book and read it. Remind yourself why you're doing what you're doing. Use these words to restore your faith and move forward.

IT ALL STARTS WITH A CLEAR VISION

This section is not only for all the authors out there who have already published and want guidance on how to sell more books. It's for those of you who continue to procrastinate on taking that first step toward publishing. What you're lacking is a clear vision of what's coming ahead. I'll show you how to create one for yourself so you can move forward with faith.

Is a Lack of Vision Holding *You* Back?

I get asked this question a lot: Will you read and critique my manuscript for me? Possibly. But not for free. Because this is an editing service—a paid service—that must be completed by a professional editor.

I find that many people request this even after they've already had two or three friends or colleagues read and critique a manuscript for them. Those people gave it a rave review, and now they're looking for ... what? Another rave review? Or maybe a criticism—a way out?

I always ask these people, "And what will happen if *I* like the book? Or what if I don't like it? Then what? Will you bring it to someone else to read and critique? Or will you finally stop procrastinating, finish writing it, have it edited and designed, and publish it once and for all?"

The only critics who *truly* matter are your readers—your customers. And the only way you'll learn what they like and don't like is to publish it and read their reviews. You'll grow and learn from there if you keep yourself open to growing and learning. Your vision will become clearer over time.

Take a Chance on Faith

Every author experiences criticism along the way. It's okay. I get five-star and three-star reviews, and even the occasional one-star review of my books online. After several years of doing this, I've grown a thicker skin and have learned that *I* have to love me and my books first—*I* have to support my vision first—and other people's approval (whether it comes or not) is extra; it doesn't make or break me anymore. Now, when someone gives me one star with an unflattering review attached to it, I simply thank them for taking the time to read and comment on my book; then I recommend another book that they may enjoy better. End of story. Move on. You'll learn to do the same over time.

Maybe, some of that comes with age. I love this stage in my life. Why? Because, in middle age, I've reached a place where I know some people like me, some don't, some people agree with me, some don't. And I can live with that. It's a peaceful place to be.

> "Some failure in life is inevitable. It is impossible to live without failing at something, unless you live so cautiously that you might as well not have lived at all—in which case, you fail by default."
> ~J. K. Rowling, 2008 Harvard Commencement Speech

In other words, you fail by default if you never publish your book. But you have a strong chance of success if you go through with it—publish it and then sell it by following the steps set out for you in this book. Just *do* it, already! Take a chance on faith.

Let These People Inspire You to Build Your Own Clear Vision

Throughout this final section in the book, I want to share some of my greatest sources of inspiration—people who have taught me to keep the faith when I was feeling down after a bad review or just plain frustrated that there were no reviews or sales at all. Every single one of these winners experienced failures, criticisms, and disappointments of their own along the way. But they kept the faith and kept working toward their respective goals. Eventually, they won over their critics. Or, in the very least, they proved them wrong.

> "The greatest revenge is massive success."
> ~Tony Robbins

If you don't have a clear vision of where you want to go with your book business right now, that's okay. Don't push it. Read through this book to get an idea of what's actually possible for you. Then ask for the specific plan that will bring you joy and success with your books. Send that prayer out into the cosmos and keep yourself open to receiving the answer. Have faith that it will come to you just as it did for the following people.

Her "Idea Moment" Came to Her Before the Actual Idea

You may have heard of Sara Blakely, the now-billionaire founder of Spanx. But are you aware of her humble beginnings and everything she went through to build her empire? I've researched this woman intently over the last few years, and her story is truly inspirational. She's one of the most accessible, down-to-earth, humorous, and likeable business leaders I've ever come across in my studies. Her story started with a simple vision as described in a CNN interview with Poppy Harlow (which is posted on YouTube for all to view for free).

Her "idea moment," as she calls it, happened *before* the actual idea for her business came to her. She was unhappy with her mundane job as a door-to-door fax machine salesperson, and she began to visualize a new life and career for herself. Her intention began simply as, "I want to invent something that I can sell to millions of people, and I want the product to make people feel good."

The invention, itself, came to her in a moment of frustration some time later. She was getting dressed for an evening out, and she couldn't find anything to wear underneath her white pants that would smooth out panty lines and hide cellulite. That's when she cut the feet out of her control-top pantyhose and put those on under her pants. This provided the "smooth canvass" she was after and helped her to look even more toned and slim. The problem was, the pantyhose rolled up her legs all night. So, she decided, then and there, that she would invent footless pantyhose to solve this issue for herself and all other women.

His Blueprint to Success Was Laid Out for Him in a Magazine Article

Whether you like Arnold Schwarzenegger's movies or agree with his political views, I think we can all agree he is a successful man—in more than one area of his life. In fact, he has conquered physical fitness, money, the movie business, *and* the political arena. But none of these roads were easy for him to travel.

Arnold came from very humble beginnings, born in a little village in Austria after World War II. He describes growing up in a country stricken by depression, alcoholism, famine, and poverty caused by Germany's defeat in that war. He always knew he wanted to get out of there; he wanted a better life for himself. But nothing about his surroundings provided any degree of hope for anything more.

During school one day, Arnold created his vision while watching a video about the successful United States of America with its tall skyscrapers, large freeways, and magnificent bridges. He fell in love with the idea of living in America and began to visualize one day living there himself. Of course, international travel was uncommon back then. Nobody had much money. So, he had no idea how he could possibly make this vision come true.

A few years later, he came across an article about Reg Park in a bodybuilding magazine titled "How Mr. Universe Became a Hercules Star." He read through it and realized this was his ticket to America: an award-winning bodybuilding career followed by a notable acting career. The whole "blue print" was laid out for him, right before his eyes. At 15 years old, Arnold became a bodybuilder with that clear vision in his mind. He worked out five or six hours per day, just as Reg had done, to progress toward his goal a little more each day.

This Man Dubbed His Calling "The Church of Freedom from Concern"

As a fellow Canadian, Jim Carrey has a special place in my heart. In one of the most inspirational speeches I've ever heard (which is posted on YouTube for all to listen to for free), he describes how the pain of his childhood became the catalyst for his own vision of success.

> "My father could have been a great comedian, but he didn't believe that that was possible for him, and so he made a conservative choice. Instead, he got a safe job as an accountant. And when I was 12 years old, he was let go from that safe job, and our family had to do whatever we could to survive. I learned many great lessons from my father, not the least of which was that you can fail at what you *don't* want. So, you might as well take a chance on doing what you love."
> ~Jim Carrey, 2014 Maharishi University of Management Commencement Address

Following his father's lay-off, Jim and his family lost their home and had to live in a van for a time. Worse yet, at age 15, he had to quit school and take a job as a janitor to help support his family. It was a traumatic time for him, to say the least.

Still, Jim could see the *positive* effect that his father's love and humour had on everyone around him—even in the most difficult of times. He saw, through his dad, a beautiful life purpose he could emulate himself. Back then, his decision to become a comedian was more about helping ease other peoples' pain—freeing them from concern—than becoming "rich and famous." Once he realized this life purpose, his vision became crystal clear to him; and he dubbed his new devotion (his "ministry") The Church of Freedom from Concern. That is how he decided he would serve the world in this lifetime. Isn't that beautiful? And look how far that vision has taken him.

She Just Didn't Want to Live *This* Way Anymore

Lisa Nichols inspires me! Because she's so real. She's so unapologetically *real*. You can pull up any number of YouTube videos of her speaking, or you can read her bestselling books, and you'll see exactly what I mean.

In the 1990s, Lisa Nichols was a single parent supporting herself and her son, Jelani, on government welfare. Her son's father had just gone to jail. One night, she experienced her version of "rock bottom" when she went to an automated teller to withdraw $20 so she could buy diapers for her son ... but there were insufficient funds in the account. Lisa ended up having to wrap her baby boy in towels for two days because she couldn't afford to buy diapers. During one of these evenings, she put her hand on his stomach and promised him, "Mommy will never be this broke or broken ever again."

Lisa's dream didn't start as a grand vision of becoming the multimillionaire public speaker and media personality she now is. It started simply as a firm decision that she wouldn't live *this* way anymore—always struggling to make ends meet. As someone who was raised in a rough part of South Central Los Angeles, she knew that *statistically* her son had a very high chance of joining a gang or ending up in prison like his father had. So, to transform their lives, she knew she would have to leave the area and seek out new influences and opportunities. That's when Lisa became an avid student of abundance and prosperity which eventually led her to becoming a teacher of abundance and prosperity for others through her company that she has aptly named Motivating the Masses.

This Woman Asked God to Give Her a Platform to Do Good

As early as four years old, Oprah Winfrey recalls standing on the back porch of her home and watching her grandmother boiling clothes because they didn't have a washing machine. Even at that early age, she told herself, "My life won't be like this. It will be better." Oprah knew she had a different calling, although that calling wasn't clear to her yet at that time.

Her vision became a little clearer years later, in her early twenties, when she was working in television. She longed to be an actress more than a news anchor or talk show host, but she was unwilling to give up a job she knew so many others wanted. So, Oprah decided she would have to be discovered somehow through her television appearances. And that's exactly how it happened for her. One day, she read what she believed was the perfect role for her inside a book, and she began visualizing herself in that role.

> **7:49 location on video:** I truly believe that thoughts are the greatest vehicle to change, power, and success in the world. Everything begins with thoughts. ... I thought up The Color Purple [film] for myself. I know this is going to sound strange to you. I read the book. I got so many copies of that book. I passed the book around to everybody I knew. If I was on the bus, I'd pass it out to people. And, when I heard that there was going to be a movie, I started talking it up for myself. I didn't know Quincy Jones or Steven Spielberg, or how on earth I would get in this movie. I'd never

acted in my life. But I felt it so intensely that I had to be a part of that movie. I just, I really do believe that I created it for myself. (Winfrey)

Later, Oprah's vision became more profound than simply wanting to be an actress. She wanted to be able to change people's lives for the better, and she realized that television gave her the most incredible platform for that influence. Before every Oprah show, she did a mental meditation—a prayer—to ensure the correct message would get across to her millions of viewers. And the "correct message" she intended to get across through each show is that we're all responsible for our own lives, no matter what is going on around us. Even in tragedy, there is always an opportunity to triumph.

He Wanted to Help Other People Escape and Feel Inspired

For many of us, watching any of the Rocky movies serves as an instant and powerful source of motivation to get up off one's butt and *achieve*! Well, the life story of the man behind those movies is even more impactful. Sylvester Stallone's road to success is a real "rags to riches" story about what's truly possible if you stay focused on a goal, and he's one of my top sources of inspiration whenever I need a mental and emotional boost.

Like Oprah, Sylvester wanted to be in the movie business since he was very young. He wasn't interested in a television career—only movies. His compelling reason for this, which had him take some extreme risks that may make other people shutter, was that he saw movies as an opportunity to help other people escape and feel inspired. Just as his Rocky movies show people what they're truly capable of and how to overcome incredible odds, so does his own drive to get the first film in that series made.

My Own Vision Has Always Been About Travel and Freedom

I started Polished Publishing Group (PPG) as a "digital publishing company" in November 2009. In retrospect, I didn't fully understand *effective* digital publishing at that time. Nearly ten years later, I can confidently say I do, and the way I run my company has evolved as a result. That's usually how it happens for people. There will be twists and turns in the road as you navigate your way toward your vision. That's okay. Just keep your eye on the goal and trust that you'll get there eventually. Enjoy the journey and all its lessons along the way. I know *I* have.

From the start, my goal has always been to operate my business in a virtual office environment, untethered from any particular geographic location. I've seen myself leading by example with my own successful books while helping others to achieve success with theirs. In my mind's eye, I visualize attending book fairs, writing conferences, and author events all around the world—networking with my cherished industry peers (e.g., authors, publishers, booksellers, agents), and posting educational/inspirational success stories about them on my YouTube channel and podcast. As time goes on, I'd much rather work with people (help each other) than compete against anyone. I see this industry evolving into one where writers now have an honest opportunity to earn a *decent* living from their life's work rather than surviving the proverbial "starving artist" lifestyle.

When I founded PPG almost a decade ago, my focus was on "polished publishing." My strategy was to help authors produce professional quality books that could stand proudly beside traditionally-published books, so these books had a better chance of selling. Helping authors with additional book sales and marketing was a secondary service I offered for a sizeable fee.

Now? I still take on publishing business. But my primary focus has shifted to "successful selling." My strategy is to respect every authors' desire for creative freedom by teaching them how to cost-effectively sell their own books, no matter who they've published through—whether that be PPG, another publisher, or independently. I do this through my blog, my books, and online courses which enables me to reach my audience from wherever I am in the world. It allows me to make my *Sales Coaching for Authors* programs affordable for everyone, no matter where you live.

Respecting others' creative freedom, in this way, gives me the creative freedom *I* desire. It allows me to travel and see this beautiful world of ours while I earn a living doing what I love to do most. That's what I've always craved for myself from the start: freedom. Creative, financial, and otherwise. FREEDOM. And I want to help others enjoy the same.

What is *Your* Vision?

If you haven't already done so, send a prayer into the universe and ask for a clear vision of success for your authorship. How will you serve your readers in a way that brings you (and them) a strong sense of fulfillment? What does your perfect writing room look like? Do you see yourself traveling the world or working from home? Can you visualize your books being adapted into film like the Harry Potter or Hunger Games book series were? If yes, who will play the staring role in these movies? Will you attend the premieres? What will you say about your books and your life when you're interviewed? Get specific with your visualizations. Have fun with it. Feel the joy you'll feel when these things happen for real.

> "All you need is your own imagination. So, use it that's what it's for. Go inside for your finest inspiration. Your dreams will open the door."
> ~Madonna, Vogue lyrics

If you still think this isn't possible for you, keep reading. This book is filled with stories of people who started with nothing except a dream and turned it into a reality despite unbelievable odds. Let their life stories act as your proof of what's possible in those moments when you're doubting everything. Keep feeding yourself these positive examples and affirmations while you work toward your goal, and trust that your faith will develop over time. Once it does, you'll be unstoppable.

WHEN YOU COME UP AGAINST RESISTANCE, STAY THE COURSE

When you come up against any resistance along the way—and you *will*—I recommend you read this chapter to remind yourself that you're in good company. You'll find it helps you feel better. Most (if not all) of today's most successful people had to overcome other people's misunderstanding, criticism, or outright opposition to their goals. In fact, even people like Guglielmo Marconi, the Italian inventor of radio communication, came up against some *serious* resistance from those closest to him.

> Marconi dreamed of a system for harnessing the intangible forces of the ether. Evidence that he did not dream in vain may be found in every radio, TV, and cell phone in the world. Moreover, Marconi's dream brought the humblest cabin and the most stately manor house side by side. It made people of every nation on earth next-door neighbors by creating a medium where news, information, and entertainment could instantly be disseminated throughout the world. It may interest you to know that Marconi's "friends" had him taken into custody, and examined in a psychopathic hospital, when he announced he had discovered a principle through which he could send messages through the air, without the aid of wires or other direct physical means of communication. (Hill, 1937)

I think it's safe to say you won't come across quite that extreme of opposition against your own book goals. (At least, I hope not!) My purpose in including Marconi's example—and all the examples listed in this chapter—is simply to show you that you're not alone when you face resistance in the future. Stay the course, as these people did, and you'll eventually fulfill your vision. You may even change the world in the process. Thank God Marconi stayed the course even after those closest to him had him committed for treatment, otherwise we may not be enjoying the benefit of his inventions today. How else would I have the freedom to run a digital publishing company without wireless communication?

Her Lawyer Thought Her Idea Was *So* Bad, He Must Be on Candid Camera

There are several videos posted on YouTube of Sara Blakely giving keynote speeches to either the National Association of Professional Women (NAPW) or The Edge Connection in Atlanta, Georgia, et cetera. I highly recommend watching all of them. She is frank about her total lack of direction in her early career—from two failed attempts at The Law School Admission Test (LSAT), a stint working as a chipmunk at Disney World (after being rejected for the Goofy role), a couple of stand-up comedy gigs, to finally settling on a job selling fax machines for an office supply company called Danka. Sara pokes fun at herself all the way through this story filled with many twists and turns, which puts the rest of us at ease by letting us know it's okay to fail along the way. Everyone does.

In fact, there were many "failures" and rejections along Sara's Spanx journey that would have stopped most people in their tracks. First of all, *nobody* understood her vision of "footless pantyhose" in the beginning; so, even finding a manufacturer who would agree to help her make a prototype was a challenge all on its own. This was because she was dealing mainly with men who couldn't see things through a woman's eyes. And that's when it dawned on her that maybe this was the whole reason why women's shapers and undergarments were so uncomfortable—because they were being created by men who had never worn them before. Luckily, this realization motivated Sara rather than discouraging her. She knew she was going to change the way women wear clothes, and she stayed true to that vision through every trial and tribulation she faced—even despite no formal business education or fashion industry experience.

Sara couldn't even find a female patent attorney in the state of Georgia, so trying to patent her "footless pantyhose" idea proved to be equally trying. Again, she found herself dealing with men who simply couldn't understand her vision. In fact, the attorney who ended up helping her later admitted that he'd initially thought her idea was *so* bad it must be a joke. While she was describing it to him in his office that first day, he kept looking around for a hidden camera because he thought he was being pranked for an episode of Candid Camera.

Finally, after several attempts, she found a hosiery mill that would work with her. Why did this one finally come around? Because the man she met with ran her idea by his two daughters; they loved it and begged him to help Sara make it. Finally, some females could see the brilliance of her vision. But that only happened due to Sara's own persistence.

This Young Man Was Thrown in Jail for Pursuing His Goal

The following quote isn't just some formulaic rhetoric that Arnold Schwarzenegger spews to his audience members during keynote speeches. He lives his own life by these words. He walks his talk every day. These five rules are exactly how he has achieved every single one of his goals:

> "Have a vision. Think big. Ignore the naysayers. Work your ass off. And give back and change the world. Because if not us, who? If not now, when?"
> ~Arnold Schwarzenegger

Arnold was faced with many naysayers all through his life, starting with his own friends and family members in Austria. For starters, none of them understood his obsession with bodybuilding because it wasn't a common sport in their part of the world. They teased the 15-year-old relentlessly about his "impossible dreams," and his worried mother even called a doctor to try to make sense of all the pictures of oiled-up muscle men on his bedroom walls. When Arnold turned 18, his abusive alcoholic father gladly sent him off to the military in the hopes it would set his son straight.

Arnold's next big obstacle was trying to figure out how to train every day within the confines of a military base. They didn't have the standard bodybuilding equipment he needed, and they controlled much of his time with military training. He decided not to let anything stop him and challenged himself to work even harder every day. When everyone else around him practically dropped dead from exhaustion in the evenings, Arnold worked out for three more hours. He even woke up earlier than everyone else to get his sit-ups and push-ups done every morning, all the while keeping his vision clear in his mind.

Then one day, he received an invitation to go to the Junior Mr. Europe competition in Stuttgart, Germany. This was his only opportunity to go because, once he turned 19, he would no longer qualify for this competition. Of course, the military would never willingly let Arnold go during basic training. So, after many sleepless nights, he decided he would have to sneak off the base and take a freight train to the event. This turned out to be a good decision in that he made it there in time to compete, and he won first prize! Unfortunately, he was caught a day later trying to sneak back onto the military base; and he was thrown in solitary confinement for several days as punishment.

Imagine the mental games Arnold's mind was playing with him as he sat in jail, pondering his future. But, somehow, he found a way to stay true to his vision even under those extreme conditions. He continued working out on the floor of his cell.

When his superiors finally released him from solitary, they verbally reprimanded him in their office at first. But things turned around when he confirmed for them that he had won the competition he'd gone AWOL to attend. Their anger then turned to pride, and they began using him as an example of strong discipline in front of his peers. They also had body building equipment built for him so he could continue working out every day. Arnold had *finally* won everyone over after three years of going it alone.

From there, he won several more European bodybuilding titles which eventually led to him receiving a literal "ticket to America" from Joe Weider at the age of 21. He trained at Gold's Gym in Los Angeles, California, under Joe's supervision and went on to become the youngest ever Mr. Olympia two years later, at the age of 23.

Next up? Become a Hollywood movie star. This goal proved just as challenging as the first with even more naysayers lined up for him to win over.

When Arnold first began meeting with agents, managers, and studio executives in the movie industry, they literally laughed at him. They all told him it would be impossible for him to become a leading man in Hollywood due to his thick German accent, his over-developed body, and his funny name that was difficult to pronounce. They told him the new "sex symbol" trend of the day was smaller men like Woody Allen, Al Pacino, and Dustin Hoffman. He was told, "Forget about it. You're a nice guy, a fit guy. Why don't you go open up a gym or health food store?" They told him the most he could hope for may be a few bit parts playing a bouncer or maybe a Nazi officer in Hogan's Heroes. That was all he should expect.

But Arnold saw more for himself. He'd already proven to himself, once before, that he could achieve a goal against all odds. He just had to keep his vision clear in his mind while he took daily action toward it. Determined to succeed, he applied the same work ethic and dedication to becoming an actor as he had used to become Mr. Olympia. He started taking acting classes, English classes, speech classes, and even accent removal classes on the side of his full-time work in construction.

Arnold got his first break in 1970 playing Hercules in a movie called Hercules in New York where they recorded another man's voice over his to hide his accent. That was followed by more little television parts and a chance to appear in one of Lucille Ball's specials. Six years later, he appeared in Stay Hungry, then The Streets of San Francisco, then Pumping Iron, et cetera. Finally, he got his big break with Conan the Barbarian—a movie fraught with difficulties and delays that didn't actually premiere in theatres until 1982.

Whenever Arnold speaks about his achievements, he highlights how his personal qualities, that the naysayers had once categorized as liabilities, eventually became his greatest assets. While on a promotional tour, the director of Conan the Barbarian told the press, "If we didn't have Arnold with all his muscles, we would have had to build one." When Arnold later starred in The Terminator, James Cameron expressed gratitude for his accent with this statement: "The 'I'll be back' line became one of the most famous movie lines in history because of Arnold's crazy accent, because he sounded like a machine when he talked."

Arnold faced similar obstacles when he ran for Governor of California years later. Of course, he eventually won that race, too. Didn't he? The rest of his story is history.

This Undiagnosed Dyslexic Started Out Earning Only $25 Per Set

As if living in poverty in a van wasn't a big enough obstacle for the teenage Jim Carrey, there were many more mountains for him to climb on his journey to success. An undiagnosed dyslexic who often struggled in school, he ended up dropping out halfway through grade 10 to help his family make ends meet. But someone without a high school diploma—or even a GED—doesn't have many job options. He could be hired for janitorial or dishwashing jobs, but that was about it. Imagine how that must have affected his self-esteem and mental health at such a young age.

Jim decided he'd might as well go to the local comedy clubs at night and work on his act for $25 per set. At least it was *some* money, and it allowed him to move toward his vision of freeing other people—perhaps even himself, at that time—from concern. It's hard to believe that his first attempts at doing impressions completely bombed. But Jim stayed the course and honed his talent, spending hours in front of the mirror to perfect his facial expressions.

In his late twenties, he finally landed a recurring role with an American sketch comedy television series called In Living Color. That gave him some national recognition, enabling him to tour and earn more money as a stand-up comedian.

Four years after his In Living Color debut, Jim Carrey completed three movies that made him a multimillionaire: Ace Ventura: Pet Detective (1994), Dumb and Dumber (1994), and The Mask (1994). Now he's a household name. But his journey there was a long one that lasted well over a decade.

Her Teachers Were Mentally Abusive and Her Family Resented Her

If you are ever given the opportunity to listen to Lisa Nichols speak about her past and all the obstacles she had to overcome to get to where she is today, take it. She is living, breathing proof that anything is possible for *anyone* who is willing to work for it. And she is one of the most inspirational authors and sought-after public speakers in the world right now.

But it wasn't always that way for her. Nothing was handed to this self-proclaimed "C Student" in life. Quite the opposite. In school, Lisa's English teacher told her she was the weakest writer she'd ever met in her entire life. That same year, she took a speech class and that teacher recommended she get a desk job and never speak in public. Can you say *cruelty*? These were supposed to be professional *teachers*—people who support and nurture their students.

But the beauty of Lisa Nichols is that she never dwelled on what negative people like that said to her, nor does she hold any grudges toward them to this day. She simply chalks their attitudes up to, "These were demotivated, sad people. Hurt people hurt other people. Sad people make other people sad. Don't take it personal."

Through these teachers and other troubled people in her community, Lisa could see that her only chance at a better life was to leave and find new sources of education and inspiration. During an interview with Tom Bilyeu, she said, "I had to be willing to not only relocate my mind but also relocate my body so I could relocate my finances, relocate my possibilities, and relocate my son's future." And this would be up to her alone since her son's father had landed in prison when their baby was only eight months old.

When Lisa became an avid student of abundance and prosperity, she didn't have a lot of support around her initially. In fact, her new focus caused some resentment and concern among her immediate family members. She told Tom, "I had to go through a window of ten years of judgement: 'You're leaving us, hanging out with white people all the time, going to all these crazy countries...' But I knew I had to be willing to allow my conviction to make me inconvenienced." That's not an easy thing to do, especially when your own family is holding meetings about you—and you're not invited to them!

During that same interview, Lisa said, "Most people want the convenience of transformation without the inconvenience that is required to make that transformation." She was willing to make those inconvenient, radical changes to transform her and her son's life—working harder, sleeping less, leaving her "tribe" to walk on her own path for a while. "The doorway to your new life is for *you* to fit through. You can't carry everybody else through it with you—trying to be their Rescue 911. You have to rescue *you* first." Lisa says she is now much more valuable to her family, and to her community, because she was willing to let them go, walk through that door alone, teach herself, learn a better way of living, and then come back and get them afterward. Her family can now see how much more valuable she is to them, too.

Her College Peers Were Jealous of Her Success and Taunted Her About It

Oprah Winfrey may have gotten some early breaks in her career, but she also had to suffer through similar resentment and criticism as Lisa Nichols did. The most hurtful taunting came from her college peers when she was a young and insecure nineteen-year-old.

> **32.35 location on video:** And I started to read. Now, I've been reading since I was three. They couldn't believe how well I read, and I was hired. There. So, when somebody said, 'Sit down and read' and they said 'Come hear this girl read!' And

someone else came, and before I knew it, there were four guys standing in the room listening to me read. And I was hired, 17 years old, in radio. At the time, I was still a senior [in high school], so I had to only work after school. So, I'd finish, get there by 3:30, and I'd do on-the-air newscasts. Well, all my friends just hated me because they're cutting grass. And, um, my sophomore year in college, someone heard me on the radio and said, 'We heard you on the radio, would you be interested in working in television.' And I turned them down three times. And the third time, I had a college professor, I said, 'They keep calling me to be on television. And I know if I do television, I'll never finish school.' So, he said, 'Don't you know that's why people *go* to school? So that somebody can keep calling them, you nitwit!' So, I went, and I interviewed for the job [in television] … I was 19 at the time, so I decided to pretend to be Barbara Walters because that's how I'd gotten into this in the first place. So, I sat there, pretending with Barbara in my head, did everything I thought she would do, and I was hired. It was amazing. As a matter of fact, it was because of the riots of the 70s that I think they were looking for minorities. They were trying to fulfill all of their quotas and programs, and so I was hired as a token and had to take the heat from my college classmates. I went to an all-black college with them calling me a token. … And I was very defensive about it because I've always had to live with the notion of other black people saying, for any amount of success that you achieve, they say, 'Oh, you're trying to be white. You're trying to talk white. You're trying to be white.' And so forth. Which is such a ridiculous notion to me since you look in the mirror every morning and you're black. There's a black face in your reflection. So, I had to live with that whole thing. … And it was very uncomfortable for me at first because when I first started as a broadcaster, I was 19. Very insecure, thrown into television, pretending to be Barbara Walters, looking nothing like her, and still going to college. So, I would do all my classes in the morning from eight to one. And in the afternoon, I'd work from two to 10 and do the six o'clock news. And would stay up and study and all that stuff, you know, until one, two, or three o'clock in the morning. Then just start the routine all over again. (Winfrey)

She obviously had an amazing work ethic from a very young age, and that has continued throughout her life. But she also had her obstacles to overcome, just like the rest of us.

This Italian Actor Couldn't Even Get Cast for a Bit Part … as an *Italian*

Sylvester Stallone was so driven by his desire to help other people escape, and to inspire them to achieve what they're capable of in life, that he was unwilling to settle for anything else. For a long time, he was the epitome of the "starving artist." He didn't want to get a "real job" because he knew if he *did*, he'd get seduced back into "the real world" and lose the hunger he had for his dream. He felt his hunger was his greatest advantage, and he turned out to be right about that.

Audition after audition, Sylvester was turned down for acting parts. He once told Tony Robbins that he was thrown out more than 1,500 times from various agents' offices in New York. In fact, he was once even turned down for a bit part as an Italian in The Godfather. He asked, "What part of me didn't pass the Italian identification aspect?" They never gave him a straight answer why. Just imagine what *that* did to his psyche!

Sylvester persisted despite all this rejection and got a few parts here and there. He also sold a script he'd written, titled Paradise Alley, for $100. That gave him some hope. But none of it ever led to solid work and his financial struggles continued. Eventually, he was *so* broke that he had to sell his beloved dog, Butkus, because he couldn't afford to feed him. In several interviews, he has said that was one of the lowest moments of his life.

One night, not long after he sold his dog (for only $25 ... *ouch!*), Sylvester watched a match between boxing legend Muhammad Ali and Chuck Wepner that inspired him to write the first draft of his future-Oscar-winning Rocky script. For him, that fight was a metaphor—not only for a man who takes his shot and goes the distance with a true champion, but who also stands up to life. That was who the character in his new script, Rocky Balboa, was to him. It is also the essence of Sylvester Stallone himself. Unfortunately, he would have to fight many more rounds to sell that script and get the movie made on his terms.

It wasn't enough for him to sell this script to a producer as he'd done with Paradise Alley; Sylvester also wanted to be cast in the leading role. Although he was able to find some producers who loved the script, nobody wanted to hire *him* as Rocky Balboa at first.

They wanted to put an established star in that role, instead—someone like Ryan O'Neal.

Back and forth, the negotiations continued. These producers went from offering him $25,000 to $100,000 to $150,000 to $175,000 to $250,000 to $330,000 for the rights to produce Rocky with a different actor in the starring role. Despite how broke he was, Sylvester kept turning them down. He knew what he *truly* wanted—which was to star in this movie—and he refused to compromise. Luckily, these producers eventually gave in. They brought their offer back down to $35,000, along with points in the movie, in exchange for casting Sylvester as the leading man. He agreed to the reduced rate and willingly assumed all risk along with them. This turned out to be a very profitable gamble because Rocky grossed $200,000,000 at the box office although it only cost them $1,000,000 to produce.

You may find it pleasing to learn that, as soon as Sylvester was paid the $35,000, he went in search of the man he'd sold his dog to. He found him and bought Butkus back from him. He even gave that man and his dog bit parts in the first Rocky movie. Doesn't that make you smile?

I Went to the Edge of the Cliff ... and It Crumbled Out from Under Me

Will Smith and Lisa Nichols often encourage others to face their fears of the unknown head on—to go to the proverbial edge of the cliff and jump. Just jump! Because on the other side of your fear of falling is where you'll find all your dreams and your bliss.

"God placed the best things in life on the other side of terror," Will assures you. "On the other side of your maximum fears are all of the best things in life."

"Your brain is designed to keep you safe. Your soul, your intuition, your human spirit is designed to make you soar," Lisa will tell you. "When you get to the edge, your brain will always tell you to step back. It's always going to tell you to step back because you could fall. It's designed to keep you safe. So, you have to be willing to play between your brain and your soul. And, on some days, you've got to just listen to your soul. You've got to leap."

When I came home from my Asian adventure in 2016, I decided to take Will's and Lisa's advice. As I mentioned in The Author's Money Tree section of this book, I didn't go back to a "real job" straightaway because I wanted to turn off the corporate noise and *really* focus on my craft. I found four personal investors to help me cover my expenses while I focused. In other words, I went to the edge of that cliff in the form of taking on significant debt without any guaranteed income coming into my household to offset it. I had faith the money would come to me in droves if I gave 100% effort to my vision and worked toward it daily.

What was the result of my little experiment? Two things happened: one, I achieved my first goal of *finally* figuring out how authors can earn a decent living from their books; but, two, before I could reach my second goal of earning a decent living from my own books, the edge of that cliff crumbled out from under me. In short, I stayed there too long, the money ran out, and then it took me another three and a half months to find decent employment. So, I didn't get a chance to jump *or* soar. Instead, I took a serious tumble that sent me on a financial rollercoaster ride for about two years. I was forced to find *two* new jobs, and work *seven* days per week, to recover from that fall and re-stabilize my finances.

It was humiliating; I'm not going to lie to you. It was so discouraging to reach such heights in my life only to fall back down so hard. You see, things had been on a financial upswing for me just before this happened. Not only had I enjoyed several trips during the previous three years; but, just before I got home from Asia, I'd also received an email from the team at TheSecret.tv informing me that my personal "Story of the Week" was going to be featured in Rhonda Byrne's upcoming book titled *How The Secret Changed My Life: Real People. Real Stories.* (You can read more about that here: https://blog.polishedpublishinggroup.com/2016/09/how-the-secret-changed-my-life/.)This was an absolute dream come true for me—yet another affirmation that all my actions and visualizations were paying off. It strengthened my faith that I *could* safely stand on the edge of that cliff. I *could* jump. And I *would* soar. It was the whole reason I decided to do it.

But then it all came crumbling down. During these past two years, I haven't had much of a social life—never mind any opportunities to travel. I haven't had much sleep, either; I've been too busy rebuilding. After much contemplation, I can now see the blessing in disguise. Being grounded in this way, after learning the key to success for authors, has strengthened my focus and improved my work ethic. Along with holding two jobs, I've also written and published 35 new books over the past two years—all without burning out or losing interest in the task at hand.

I have an energy that I didn't have before because <u>I know how to do this now</u>. I know it's possible, so I'm perfectly okay with doing the necessary work. By taking that time to focus solely on my vision, I gained something far greater than an immediate increase in my personal book sales. I came away with more stamina—an even *stronger* faith—than I had before. And that's what this whole book is about: developing one's faith to a point where you'll be able to overcome any obstacle you face. Because there will always be obstacles and difficulties to contend with. You're going to make mistakes along the way. If you want to succeed in life, you have to be *willing* to fail. Will Smith put it perfectly when he said this:

> **0:01 location on video:** Fail early. Fail often. Fail forward. It's always a little bit frustrating to me when people have a negative relationship with failure. Failure is a massive part of being able to be successful. You have to get comfortable with failure. You have to actually seek failure. Because failure is where all of the lessons are.
>
> When you go to the gym and you work out, you're actually seeking failure. You want to take your muscles to the point where you get to failure because that's where the adaptation is. That's where the growth is.
>
> Successful people fail a lot. They fail a whole lot more than they succeed, but they extract the lessons from the failure, and they use that—they

use the energy, and they use the wisdom—to come around to the next phase of success.

You've got to take a shot. You have to live at the edge of your capabilities. You've got to live where you're almost certain that you're going to fail. (Smith)

That's how you succeed. You already know this instinctively because that's how we all learned to walk when we were babies—by *failing* and falling, over and over again, until the day finally came when we could stand on our own two feet.

So, go to the edge of that cliff. Jump. Soar. Or, fall flat on your face as I did. Own it. Learn from it. Apologize and fix it, if the situation calls for it. Then move forward with increased faith.

No matter what, you'll be fine so long as you get back up again and keep moving forward. I can assure you that I'm fine. I'm still here. And I'm still willing and able to fail forward toward my version of success.

What Are You Telling Yourself About *Your* Obstacles?

You might be telling yourself, "Well, *they* can all do it, but I can't because…." And your mind may be feeding you all kinds of excuses and seemingly legitimate reasons why. If that's the case, I invite you to delve further into the study of faith. Read the books and watch the videos of the people I've introduced you to here. You'll begin to see that they're just like you; you're just like them.

> "Nothing was ever in any man that is not in you; no man ever had more spiritual or mental power than you can attain, or did greater things than you can accomplish. You can become what you want to be."
> ~Wallace D. Wattles

It will not happen overnight. In fact, it may take months or even years to accomplish your goals. But time doesn't really matter when you're doing what you love, does it? Because when you're doing what you love, it doesn't feel like work at all.

HOW MUCH TIME WILL IT TAKE?

How much time it takes to reach your dream is dependent on how much deliberate action, focused thought, and dedicated faith you feed it on a consistent basis. As I mentioned in section one of this series, it took Joanna Penn five years to transition into being a full-time writer and another four to earn a six-figure income from it. By contrast, it took Amanda Hocking about two years to transition from an $18,000 annual income, earned from taking care of severely disabled people, to becoming a millionaire from self-publishing her paranormal fiction series.

Everyone's journey to success is a little different, so I can't give you a definitive answer on how long it will take you. I can only show you case studies and share other people's strategies with you. They all seem to follow a similar formula as you can see by reading their stories.

It Took a Little Over Two Years for Her Invention to be Recognized Nationally

From the time Sara Blakely first cut the feet out of her control-top pantyhose, through the process of getting the prototype made, coming up with the perfect name of Spanx, designing her logo and packaging, to finally launching her product in Neiman Marcus stores was a two-year period. This was all done in her spare time, on weekends and weekday evenings, while she continued working full-time for Danka.

Some people may think that, once her product was in Neiman Marcus, it must have been smooth sailing from there. Nothing could be further from the truth. According to Sara, that's when the *real* work began, and she had to ensure the product was moving so the retailers would keep it in-store. She didn't have any money for advertising, so she had to rely on her own work ethic and sales abilities to ensure people kept buying Spanx.

Sara continued visualizing her goals while working toward them, and one of her top visualizations was being interviewed by Oprah about her invention. She sent a basketful of her products to The Oprah Winfrey Show and kept the faith that this would provide her with the big break she needed. It certainly did. Oprah named Spanx as one of her "favourite things" in November of 2000—a little more than two years after Sara first invented it. Then, and only then, did she quit her full-time job at Danka. It took another decade of hard work for Sara Blakely to be recognized as a self-made billionaire in *Forbes* magazine.

His First Goal Took Six Years to Achieve and His Second Took 12

Arnold Schwarzenegger's vision began to develop very early in his life, when he first saw that video of America in school at around the age of 10. But he didn't set a concrete plan as to how he would get to America until he was 15 years old and read that article about Reg Park; so, I'll start his official count-down from age 15.

It took Arnold until he was 21 years old to achieve his first goal of moving to America. That's six solid years. And it took 12 years, from his first role in Hercules in New York in 1970, to when he got his big break in the movie business with Conan the Barbarian in 1982.

Arnold is a role model for so many things—two of them being patience and tenacity. He *never* gave up, no matter how long it took him to reach his goals. That's why he eventually succeeded at all of them. So, if you ever come across someone who is criticizing *your* goals with, "It's taking too long. That must be a sign it won't happen for you," just remember Arnold's example. Ignore the naysayers who think you should give up. Adjust your course a bit whenever you have to. But never quit.

He Attracted $10,000,000 to Himself Within Three Years

When Jim Carrey finally landed his recurring role on the television show In Living Color, that may have been the first time he was able to see past his lifetime of financial struggles. Because, as he told Oprah Winfrey during an interview in February of 1997, that was around the time he made his first big financial wish. He told her that he used to spend evenings at the scenic overlook up on Mulholland Drive in Los Angeles. While there, he would visualize having movie directors interested in him and people that he respected telling him that they liked his work.

At this time, he also wrote himself a cheque for $10,000,000 "for acting services rendered" and gave himself three years, until Thanksgiving 1995, to make this financial wish come true. He kept that cheque in his wallet as he continued to visualize his dreams every night. Jim told Oprah, "Just before Thanksgiving 1995, I found out that I was going to make $10,000,000 on the movie Dumb and Dumber."

To which Oprah replied, "Visualization works if you work hard."

And Jim agreed, "You can't just visualize and then go eat a sandwich."

The most beautiful part of Jim Carrey's story is that, when his father passed away, he put that cheque into his casket with him. It had been his father's greatest wish for Jim to realize their shared dream of becoming a great comedian; that man had been one of his son's biggest cheerleaders through it all.

She Grew Her Bank Account from $11.42 to $62,500 in Three and a Half Years

In 1996, Lisa Nichols was a struggling single mom on government assistance, with only $11.42 in her bank account. By 2016, twenty years later, she was a multimillionaire entrepreneur. Along that winding road to long-term success, she accomplished many other short-term goals.

One of Lisa's short-term goals had to do with reframing her relationship with money—how to earn it, how to keep it, how to grow it—so she would never be that broke or broken again. She did this by scaling back the unnecessary expenses in her life (e.g., going out for dinner, getting her nails done) and putting that money into a savings account each pay day, instead. For three and a half years, Lisa invested in herself in this way, increasing the percentage she saved by 5% each month. This was how she increased her bank account balance from $11.42 to $62,500 and was able to fund her dream of motivating others to improve their lives as she had improved her own. Back then, she started by motivating teenagers. Now, she motivates the masses!

It Took Her One Decade to Turn Her Dream into Reality

Oprah may have started her television career at the young age of nineteen, but it took another thirteen years before The Oprah Winfrey Show was nationally syndicated in 1986—shortly after she was cast as Sofia in the movie The Color Purple. Considering she had wanted to be an actress since at least her early twenties, it took her around one decade of work and visualizing to make that dream come true for herself.

He Lived in Poverty for Eight Years Until His Big Break Came

Sylvester Stallone was 30 years old when the first Rocky movie was launched in theatres. But he'd already been trying to break into movies for several years at that point. Based on his IMDb webpage, his first role was in "a picture story at an LSD party on the beach" in 1969 called The Square Foot. After that, he was hired for a few minor roles as either a "stud" or a "thug" in various other films until, at long last, his Rocky dream came true in 1976. But it was a long haul for Sylvester, and he lived in poverty through all of it.

It Has Taken Me 25 Years of Trial and Error to Write This Book

Since as far back as I can remember, I've wanted to be an author, but not just any old author. I've wanted to be a *bestselling* author. It was a long and educational journey to the achievement of this goal that, once realized, still didn't allow me to earn a living from my writing. That was rather anticlimactic after putting in so much time and effort.

In 2013, I wrote and published my first official bestseller, titled *How to Publish a Book in Canada ... and Sell Enough Copies to Make a Profit!*, that discussed the merits of professional book publishing. With close to 20 years' experience in the industry, I had a strong understanding of the pros and cons of each book publishing business model (e.g., traditional trade publishing, "hybrid" supported self-publishing, and "vanity" self-publishing), and I knew what it took to create a bestseller. Still, my faith in the average author's ability—including my own—to earn a decent *living* from writing was still weak. My results reflected that frail confidence in all areas.

Three years ago, I took a hiatus from my disillusioned dream to clear my head. When I returned home from my Asian "eat pray love" working holiday six months later, I felt refreshed and ready to try again. That's when I changed my focus from earning some fruitless title to earning a decent living from my craft. I realized that my goal—my true passion—had always been about *freedom* and *travel*. And as long as I had to work full-time elsewhere to earn a living, then my freedom to travel would remain limited by someone else's rules and expectations.

Once I homed in on the *true* essence of my dream, I was able to focus and find the solutions that had long eluded me. It has taken me 25 years of trial and error to write this book. But that's okay. I've never felt more exhilarated than I do today!

How Long Will It Take You?

As you can see, from reading all the examples in this chapter, everyone's road to success is a little different. The time it takes to achieve a goal can vary. How long will it take you? I don't have an answer for you. My only advice is to never give up. Find your own passion as an author, and then work toward it each and every day. Your sense of purpose will keep you energized and feeling enthusiastic about your dream.

SUCCESS LEAVES CLUES (WORK ETHIC AND SLEEP HABITS)

I am sharing with you the final summary of a book published in 1910 by Wallace D. Wattles before I return to our case studies to share their respective work ethics and sleep habits with you. I think you'll agree, once you read this, they are all indeed following this formula. If it can work for them, it can work for you.

> There is a thinking stuff from which all things are made, and which, in its original state, permeates, penetrates, and fills the interspaces of the universe.
>
> A thought in this substance produces the thing that is imaged by the thought.
>
> Man can form things in his thought, and by impressing his thought upon formless substance can cause the thing he thinks about to be created.
>
> In order to do this, man must pass from the competitive to the creative mind; otherwise he cannot be in harmony with the Formless Intelligence, which is always creative and never competitive in spirit.
>
> Man may come into full harmony with the Formless Substance by entertaining a lively and sincere gratitude for the blessings it bestows upon him. Gratitude unifies the mind of man with the intelligence of Substance, so that man's thoughts are received by the Formless. Man can remain upon the creative plane only by uniting himself

with the Formless Intelligence through a deep and continuous feeling of gratitude.

Man must form a clear and definite mental image of the things he wishes to have, to do, or to become; and he must hold this mental image in his thoughts, while being deeply grateful to the Supreme that all his desires are granted to him. ... Too much stress cannot be laid on the importance of frequent contemplation of the mental image, coupled with unwavering faith and devout gratitude. This is the process by which the impression is given to the Formless, and the creative forces set in motion.

The creative energy works through the established channels of natural growth, and of the industrial and social order. All that is included in his mental image will surely be brought to the man who follows the instructions given above, and whose faith does not waver. What he wants will come to him through the ways of established trade and commerce.

In order to receive his own when it shall come to him, man must be active; and this activity can only consist in more than filling his present place. ... And he must do, every day, all that can be done that day, taking care to do each act in a successful manner. He must give to every man a use value in excess of the cash value he receives, so that each transaction makes for more life; and he must so hold the Advancing Thought that the impression of increase will be communicated to all with whom he comes into contact. (Wattles, 1910)

Let's use sunlight as an analogy for a moment. If it is spread thin, it can brighten up a room and warm the air. But if you focus it onto one spot with a magnifying glass, it can cause an intense enough heat to start a fire. Its power becomes much stronger with more focus. The same can be said for the level of focus these individuals each gave to their own dreams—and to the level of success they were each able to achieve as a result of that intense focus.

> **2:48 location on video:** I realize that to have the level of success that I want to have is difficult to spread it out and do multiple things. It takes such a desperate, obsessive focus. You've really got to focus with all of your fibre, and all of your heart, and all of your creativity. (Smith2)

Will Smith isn't the only one who advocates intense focus. Here's what Napoleon Hill has to say about it.

> "Your ability to use the principal of autosuggestion will depend, very largely, upon your capacity to *concentrate* upon a given *desire* until that desire becomes a *burning obsession*."
> ~Napoleon Hill

In other words, if your family members start telling you, "I'm worried about you. You seem a little obsessed," then smile to yourself. Because you're probably on track to achieving great things.

She Spent *Countless* Hours on the Road Promoting Her Brand

Sara Blakely is a workhorse. I'm unable to find specific information regarding her sleep habits, but everything I *can* find on her tells me she worked her butt off daily—

and still does—to ensure her company's success. As it is with most start-ups, she had to be and do everything in the beginning. She was the inventor, manufacturer, sales person, fulfillment and shipping clerk, travel coordinator, marketer, et cetera, while she ran her company out of her apartment for the first couple of years.

Once Sara was able to hire a bit of staff to manage the administrative office work for her, she spent the next couple of years on the road. Seven days per week, she visited the Neiman Marcus stores that carried her products and promoted her Spanx brand to their customers in person. She also continued to cold call other retailers and media outlets at this time. Sara was absolutely determined to ensure her own success, so she left nothing to chance. She held morning rallies with the staff at all these stores to get them pumped up about her product—which was the equivalent of building a sales force that wasn't on her payroll. All across the country, these retail employees eventually became her biggest Spanx advocates along with her own paid staff.

To give you an idea of how much work Sara had to do, each and every day, as she drove around the country selling her products in-store, this was back in the time when nobody had iPhones, iPads, or Blackberries. It was also at a time when the MapQuest website was just becoming popular; so, that was the tool she had to use on each hotel's computer to try to find all the locations she would be driving to each day. She spent a lot of time alone on the road. It was no easy task to build her company, but the passion she felt for her dream carried her through.

This Man Says "Sleep Faster" to Those Who Think They Need Eight Hours

In response to people who try to tell him they don't have the time to do everything they want to do in a day, Arnold Schwarzenegger always replies, "There are 24 hours in a day. You sleep for six of those. That gives you 18 hours to fit everything in." And to the people who try to correct him by saying they need eight hours of sleep every night, he always says, "Sleep faster." I love that line. It makes me smile every time I hear him say it.

Arnold used every last minute of the 18 hours he had available to him every day. *Every* day. When he came to the USA, he continued training five hours a day. To earn his living, he worked as a brick-layer on the side. He went to college and worked to improve his English skills. Plus, he took acting classes every night from 8 PM to midnight. He did that every day to show the Universe how serious he was about achieving his dreams. Look where that got him.

He Worked All Day and Well into the Night for Weeks on End

Jim Carrey's dad first took him to a Yuk Yuk's comedy club in Toronto when he was 15 years old, encouraging him to participate in open mic night. The two of them had written his first comedy act together. That evening, the owner of the club heckled him to the point where Jim almost gave up on stand-up comedy altogether; he didn't return there for two full years. During this hiatus, his patient father kept encouraging him to go back, and they worked together to hone his act.

At age 17, Jim gave stand-up another *serious* try at Yuk Yuk's. This time, he did quite well with his impressions in particular—which makes sense considering he had spent untold hours perfecting them in front of his mirror at home. How many hours did he work on his craft? I found the answer I was searching for in a Rolling Stone article titled "Jim Carrey: Bare Facts and Shocking Revelations" via this one, concise sentence:

> The Carrey who would spend eight hours before a set of mirrors perfecting faces, the Carrey who can't stop himself from working all day and well into the night for weeks on end, is no stranger to darkness and compulsion. (Schruers, 1995)

This level of passion and work ethic is what catapulted Jim Carrey to levels of success he could only have imagined at age 15. Maybe, in some twisted way, that Yuk Yuk's club owner did the teenage a favour but heckling him in such a harsh manner that evening. Perhaps, that made Jim work even harder than he otherwise would have. The rewards for doing so were great.

This Single Parent Found a Way to Ensure Her Son's Bright Future

As a single parent, Lisa Nichols had less time on her hands than child-free individuals do. But she *still* found a way to do the work that was necessary to relocate her and her son's future.

> "*I* am my rescue. Nobody else."
> ~Lisa Nichols

I wish I'd read Lisa's story back when I was a single parent. My son and I may have had more opportunities/luxuries in our lives had I thought, for even a minute, that was possible for us. I now know it *is* possible no matter who you are, no matter what your circumstance is. Lisa is living, breathing proof of it. And she totally hits the mark when she talks about why her example is so powerful for others who are clinging to any shame or regret they may feel about things from the past: "Your story is not meant to be your fortress; your story is meant to be your fuel. The beauty of me being one of the top one percent earners in America is that I was once on government assistance. It wouldn't be a big deal if my family was rich."

Getting to where she is today took *years* of dedication, work, and sacrifice. She started out by using her bedroom closet as her office for the first four years. She used the clip hangers normally used for dress pants to hang all her client files in this little closet office. Back then, she worked full-time at Los Angeles Unified School District while her son was at daycare during the day. Her work day started at 8 AM. After a nine-hour day, she'd pick Jelani up and take him home where she'd enjoy a 30-minute dinner break with him at six o'clock. Then Lisa would work on her own business from six-thirty to midnight every evening. Her son would play beside her while she worked until it was his bedtime.

If Lisa's work day started at 8 AM, that means she was getting up at around 6:30 or 7 AM to get ready each day. She was living off around six and a half to seven hours of sleep every night.

When Jelani was school age, Lisa put him into a private school that allowed her to take him with her whenever she travelled for work. The school would send homework with him on the road; Lisa would help him with that homework in the evenings and then send it back to the school by FedEx®. This woman worked her ass off to fund her own dream and ensure her son's bright future. Ask Jelani if he feels he missed out on anything due to her work ethic, and I'm sure he'll tell you no. He knows just how much he has gained from it.

This Woman Feels Most Comfortable Working 14 to 16 Hours Per Day

Two chapters ago, you read Oprah Winfrey's own words about the hours she put into school, homework, and work during her senior high school and college years. She has continued that work ethic to this day.

> **1:02:20 location on video:** "14-hour days. 15. A 12-hour day is a short day for me. I feel like, after a 12-hour day, what am I going to do with the rest of my day? I get home, I don't know what to do with myself because I have all of this time left over. I don't know what to do. So, really, I feel most comfortable working 14 to 16 hours. Because then at least I can go home, usually I take a bubble bath. I love bubbles. That's the one big luxury I've given myself, is that now that I have attained some material success, I will use an entire half a bottle of bubble bath at one time. Really extravagant." (Winfrey)

This woman's work ethic is much like Arnold Schwarzenegger's in that she seems to average only six hours of sleep each night. Do the math. If she's working 16 hours per day, and she's spending another two hours on things like dinner and commuting to/from work, that leaves six hours for sleep. She obviously loves what she does to be able to maintain this schedule.

His Three-Day Writing Frenzy Earned $200,000,000

I haven't been able to find any articles or videos specific to his sleep habits. But, whenever Sylvester Stallone talks about watching that match between boxing legend Muhammad Ali and Chuck Wepner, and then feeling inspired to write that first draft of Rocky, he speaks of it being a passionate "writing frenzy" over a period of three days. That three-day writing frenzy, combined with several more months of passionate activity, ultimately earned $200,000,000 at the box office. Three focused, inspired writing days. Barely any sleep. $200,000,000.

She Danced Her Way to Becoming the Most Watched Woman in the World

As a teenager in the 1980s, I was obsessed with everything about Madonna from her fashion to her music videos. I was especially mesmerized whenever I watched her dance. Years later, when I saw a documentary about her titled Driven: Madonna (https://www.youtube.com/watch?v=95hPbDHDAIc), I learned I wasn't the only one who felt this way about her. So many others were equally hypnotized by her energy on the dance floor—even her high school teachers. When she took to the floor at high school dances, people would clear a space so they could all stand around and watch her. And Madonna loved putting on a show for them.

In this documentary, a guidance counsellor from Madonna's high school, named Nancy Mitchell, talks about how she worked harder than any of the other students did: "The thing I believe that set Madonna apart from many of the other talented kids in school was that she worked longer and harder at her dance. She was the student who got in the car, drove 25 miles to Detroit while all of the other kids were maybe out goofing around, and she was doing dance and practicing for endless hours." Other teachers were convinced Madonna would one day become a professional dancer on Broadway. They all knew she was going *somewhere* great, wherever that may be.

Madonna would go to clubs in Detroit with some of her dance teachers in the evenings. There, she got exposed to new dance moves, people, and lifestyles. After high school, she followed her favourite ballet instructor and mentor, Christopher Flynn, to the University of Michigan on a dance scholarship. This is where she met Whitley Setrakian who became her college roommate. Even Whitley describes the same drive and work ethic that Nancy Mitchell mentioned earlier: "A night after we'd been out dancing and got home at two or three in the morning, she'd be up at eight o'clock in the morning, back out the door, and in the dance department." Madonna was truly disciplined and focused on becoming a professional dancer.

That was, at least, until she became bored with it. Madonna didn't like wasting time, so the idea of spending four years to get a degree was becoming less and less attractive to her. She loved *attention* more than dance itself. She loved being watched and performing for others. So, she decided to move to New York City where she could make a much bigger mark on the world than she ever could in Detroit, Michigan. It was there that Madonna developed her vision to become a world renown entertainer—to become the most famous (most "watched") woman in the world. She put the same level of energy and focus into her new passion as she'd always put into dance, and it obviously paid off.

With Madonna, it was never "I'm going to do this" or "I'm going to be this." Right from the start, it was "I *am* this already." Ask people who knew her back then, and they'll say she lived her vision into existence very quickly by acting as though it was already reality.

As a teenager in the 1980s, I was (and still am) so grateful to Madonna for pursing her dream of being watched. I love the beautiful alchemy of her dream—that someone who others love watching also loves being watched by them. That's the power of love, right there. In my opinion, Madonna's success epitomizes the power of *love*.

His Legacy Is the Epitome of Greatness

If you love reading and watching biographies as much as I do, then you'll love JFK: Like No Other. Despite the fact that John Fitzgerald "Jack" Kennedy came from one of America's wealthiest families, all early indicators showed there was *no* reason why this man should have become the 35th President of the United States. And, despite the financial help he got from his father, plus the campaign help he got from all his family members, it still would never have happened without his own focused work ethic and love of politics.

This person suffered from *serious* health problems that would have stopped most people in their tracks, giving them legitimate excuses to rest rather than push forward:

scarlet fever, whooping cough, ongoing digestive ailments caused by colitis, Addison's disease, and chronic back pain. In fact, over his lifetime, JFK received the Catholic sacrament of last rites on four different occasions. That's how sick he was. Add to that the fact that he was filthy stinking rich by inheritance; he never *had* to work a day in his life if he didn't want to.

But JFK was driven and focused on success. Some say he lived his life as though he knew his time was limited, making the most out of each and every day. I believe that's the number one reason he reached the heights he reached during his short life.

In between his bedridden hospital stays, Jack travelled the world, attended Harvard University, and wrote a thesis titled *Appeasement at Munich* that was later published as *Why England Slept*. The book went on to become a bestseller and showed his early interest in, and understanding of, the global political arena. JFK's poor health made it near impossible for him to get past military doctors, so his father had to pull some strings for him to be able to join the navy. This enabled him to take command of a PT boat which led to him becoming a war hero—another impressive credential toward his future political career, but an experience that exacerbated his back problems. From that time forward, JFK needed a back brace and strong medications to manage his pain for the rest of his life.

It's hard to believe now but, when John Kennedy first entered politics, he resembled a scrawny teenager and was a shy, unpolished public speaker. He had to work at improving his public image daily, all while privately managing his health issues. To accomplish this feat, he campaigned from sunrise to midnight each day, climbing the stairs of three-decker buildings to knock on doors and talk to people, all while wearing his canvas-covered steel back brace. Most people would struggle to manage that pace with perfect health. That's what makes JFK's story so inspirational to me, despite all his reported sexual transgressions. His legacy—his image—is the epitome of what it takes to achieve greatness. Jack apparently kept up this pace to the very end of his life.

Writing During His Commute Earned This Author $450,000 in One Year

I can't find any articles specific to Mark Dawson's sleep habits. But I did come across one of his podcasts (SPF-076: The Science of Sleep and How It Can Help Your Writing Career – with Dr. Anne Bartolucci) that discusses the importance of sleep for creative minds, and how a brain needs adequate sleep to function well enough to be able to create anything. That said, what exactly constitutes "an adequate-enough sleep" that will allow you to be as productive and creative as someone like Mark?

> How does he maintain such a high release-rate? By using his four-hour daily commute to London to write thousands of words a day. As soon as he sits down on the train and opens up his laptop, he's writing solidly until it's time to get off. (McGregor, 2017)

For whatever reason, so many of us have this misguided notion that *everyone* needs eight hours of sleep per night in order to function properly during the day. But, according to Dr. Anne Bartolucci, sleep needs actually vary between individuals. While she says she needs around eight hours of sleep each night, she acknowledges that her husband only needs around six. In fact, if he gets too much sleep for him (e.g., eight hours per night) for too many days in a row, it turns into insomnia.

Obviously, if Mark Dawson was having to commute four hours each day for work, plus working an eight-hour day, he was living off—and being highly productive on—only around six hours of sleep per night. I say that because you have to give him at least another six waking hours per day for meals, family time, and all the additional activities involved in successful book publishing.

Her Frenzy of Focused Activity Precipitated Million-dollar Book Sales

I've often wondered why Amanda Hocking was able to become a multimillionaire so quickly compared to most other independent authors. Then, one day, it hit me as I was researching the work ethic and sleep habits of my most cherished mentors-from-afar. I noticed something I hadn't noticed before, and I would like to share it with you here. It is a portion of the Ed Pilkington article in The Guardian, titled "Amanda Hocking, the writer who made millions by self-publishing online," that I've mentioned beforehand.

> In 2009 she went into overdrive. She was frantic to get her first book published by the time she was 26, the age Stephen King was first in print, and time was running out (she's now 27). So while holding down a day job caring for severely disabled people, for which she earned $18,000 a year, she went into a Red Bull-fuelled frenzy of writing at night, starting at 8pm and continuing until dawn.

> Once she got going, she could write a complete novel in just two or three weeks. By the start of 2010, she had amassed a total of 17 unpublished novels, all gathering digital dust on the desktop of her laptop. (Pilkington, 2012)

This frenzy of focused activity—working all day at her full-time job followed by writing all evening and late into the night—seems to be what precipitated the mass sales of her books once she published them a year later. Coincidence? Maybe. Maybe not.

Sleep Doesn't Create Energy. *Faith* Does.

My conclusion, from all my research, is that there is something ethereal to this sleep thing—or, specifically, this *obsessed* level of focused productivity during one's waking hours. The more I study other successful people, the more I realize prayer is received by God (or the Universe, or whatever you call it) through your *actions* more so than your thoughts. It is only when you combine focused action, grateful thoughts, and a strong feeling of faith together that your prayers are fully heard and finally answered.

> "The answer to prayer is not according to your faith while you are talking, but according to your faith while you are working."
> ~Wallace D. Wattles

We all need enough sleep. But energy doesn't come from enough sleep; it comes from feeling a strong desire for something and a faith that you can achieve it. I learned that firsthand, over these past two years, when I published 35 books while working two jobs simultaneously. Where that pace would have burned me out in the past, I can easily maintain it now—because I know how to do this now. I know it's possible. I have faith.

> **15:20 location on video:** We're not made for work. Work's made for us. What we've got to do is find out what we *love*, and then you have to do it because you *love* it. ... See, when people quit—like Three Feet from Gold—they weren't in love with that idea. They were going after the money. It wasn't the idea that motivated them; it was the money that motivated them, and that's why they quit. ... That's one of the big problems with people when they set goals. They set a goal to do what they think they can do. Well, there's no inspiration in that. It's got to be what you *want* to do. ... When you're going after your heart's desire, you don't quit. ... You see, you don't *get* energy. All the energy there ever was or ever will be is omnipresent. It's evenly present in all places at the same time. You don't *get* energy; you *release* energy. You're just an instrument that energy flows through. Desire is the triggering mechanism that releases the energy. When you've got the desire, you've got the energy. When you haven't got any desire, you haven't got any energy. (Proctor, 2017)

This is what Wallace D. Wattles is referring to when he says you must "do each act in a *successful* manner." Your dream needs to inspire you. The actions you take need to energize you—and they *will* when they are infused with grateful thoughts and a strong feeling of faith. When you combine these three things—action, thought, and faith—in most every act you take toward your dream, then most every act you take will be successful. Your dream as a whole will be successful.

I Have Far More Energy Due to This Change in my Sleeping Habits

My mother is a wonderful, caring person. She's also a nurse whose health advice I've heeded all my life. My mother was (and still is) a strong advocate of a "good night's sleep." But, looking back, that was taken to extremes when I was a child. I was in bed at 8 PM and slept for 12 hours until 8 AM seven days per week. She also made sure I had a two-hour nap every afternoon. That means I was asleep for 14 hours per day, every day, for the first five years of my life. I slept more than half my life away at that time.

Long sleep hours—at least eight hours every night, if not more, combined with afternoon naps on the weekends—continued well into my twenties, thirties, and even early forties. I did this out of habit because getting "enough sleep" had been drilled into my mind as an important part of healthy living. Whenever I felt tired, I assumed it was because I hadn't gotten a good enough sleep the night before. So, I'd try to sleep even *more* to make up for it.

A little while ago, something clicked for me: I've been chronically tired for most of my life.

This clicked for me when I *stopped* feeling chronically tired around one and a half years ago—when I was forced to work two jobs, seven days per week, to restore my finances. One of my jobs was working with the morning crew for a local drug store chain. My weekend shifts ran from 5 AM to 9 AM. My weekday shifts, for my regular full-time job, started at 7:30 AM downtown which meant I had to leave my house by at least 7 AM for the commute.

I remember the first time my alarm went off at 4 AM for that first morning crew shift. I was shocked by it and thought, "I'm *never* going to be able to do this." But, out of necessity, I did it. I got used to it. And, by the time my shifts were over, I had tons of energy and the whole day ahead of me to write my books.

About a year ago, I decided to set my alarm for 4 AM every single day of the week. I do my best writing first thing in the morning, so I decided to put *me* first every single day and write for two hours before getting into the shower to get ready for work. I continue to write in the evenings whenever I can, too.

I've gotten my sleep down to between six and seven hours every night, and I've completely cut out afternoon naps. I have *way* more energy for doing it. I'm a far more productive individual because of this change in my sleeping habits. I thank God for this "accidental" discovery!

Recommended Resources on Sleep Habits

Get More Hours In Your Day:
http://www.keypersonofinfluence.com/get-more-hours-in-your-day/ "Having looked at successful people like Sir Richard Branson, I found that many are members of the elite 5am Club who begin their day at 5 in the morning."

Is sleeplessness REALLY the key to Donald's success? Researchers are baffled after Trump's doctor praised the president's four-hour sleep cycle:
https://www.dailymail.co.uk/health/article-

5284457/Donald-Trump-sleeps-four-hours-night-wise.html "'How does somebody that's sleeping 12 and 14 hours a day compete with someone that's sleeping three or four?' Trump said in 2009."

I Decided to Sleep for 4 Hours a Day, See What Happened: https://www.youtube.com/watch?v=lbFzL-0pEeU "If your life is like one big to-do list that you just can't seem to keep up with, then polyphasic sleep is probably for you. All jokes aside, I definitely became more productive, and I have a lot of spare time that allows me to do everything I want and even more."

IT'S TIME TO MAKE *YOUR* DREAM COME TRUE

The beauty of being a writer in this digital age is that writing *is* selling in the online world. It's as though the Internet was built just for us writers, isn't it? We are precious commodities to online marketers and other business people who wish to hire copywriters and ghostwriters to help them publish blog posts and books. Best of all, we can write and publish our own blog posts and books—and *finally* earn a decent living doing what we love to do. It's possible!

Your dream may resemble mine in some ways, or you may be inspired to follow an entirely different path than me. My best advice is to follow your own intuition and have faith in your ability to achieve your heart's desire. I hope the tools and guidance provided throughout this book is most useful to you along your journey; and I hope you'll share your success story with my blog subscribers in a guest post some day. I welcome that.

Whenever you come across obstacles that test your faith along the way, please read this book again. Use it to restore your faith by reading the stories of all these people who succeeded against incredible odds. They're just like you. You're just like them. Jim Carrey said it best when he said this:

> "Your imagination is always manufacturing scenarios, both good and bad. And the ego tries to keep you trapped in the multiplex of the mind. Our eyes are not only viewers; they're also projectors that are running a second story over the picture

that we see in front of us all the time. Fear is writing that script, and the working title is 'I'll Never Be Enough.' ... No matter what you gain, ego will not let you rest. It will tell you that you cannot stop until you've left an indelible mark on the earth, until you've achieved immortality. How tricky is this ego that it would tempt us with the promise of something we already possess? Relax, and dream up a good life."
~Jim Carrey, 2014 Maharishi University of Management Commencement Address

In other words, there's nothing at all to fear. There's never any reason to procrastinate. Write your book. Publish it. Sell it. Enjoy the ride! I hope this creates untold wealth for you.

BIBLIOGRAPHY

AccelerationPartners®. (2014, November 5). *HOW DOES AFFILIATE MARKETING WORK?* Retrieved from Affiliate Marketing 101: Part I: https://www.accelerationpartners.com/blog/affiliate-marketing-101-part-i

Alter, A. (2016, March 21). *James Patterson Has a Big Plan for Small Books*. Retrieved from The New York Times: https://www.nytimes.com/2016/03/22/business/media/james-patterson-has-a-big-plan-for-small-books.html

Altman, I. (2015, December 1). *Top 10 Business Trends That Will Drive Success In 2016*. Retrieved from Forbes: https://www.forbes.com/sites/ianaltman/2015/12/01/top-10-business-trends-that-will-drive-success-in-2016/#5b06ccc358ea

Clarke, A. (2018). In *SEO 2018: Learn Search Engine Optimization With Smart Internet Marketing Strategies. [Kindle version].* United States: Simple Effectiveness Publishing. Available from Amazon.com.

Dawson, M. (2016, May 27). *SPF-013: Masterclass: A detailed look at a book launch – With Mark Dawson*. Retrieved from Self-Publishing Formula (The Self-Publishing Show): http://selfpublishingformula.libsyn.com/spf-013-how-to-launch-a-book-a-detailed-look-at-mark-dawsons-recent-book-launch

Friedman, M. (n.d.). *The Power of Publicity for Your Book*. Retrieved from News and Experts (formerly EMSI Public Relations): http://newsandexperts.com/wp-content/uploads/2014/03/Power-of-Publicity-for-Your-Book.pdf

Hill, N. (1937). *Think and Grow Rich*. United States of America: Meriden, Conn. | Ralston Society.

LaRocca, M. (2019, January 16). *Finding the Best Way to Write*. Retrieved from PPG Publisher's Blog: https://blog.polishedpublishinggroup.com/2019/01/finding-the-best-way-to-write/

Lee, K. (2016, March 21). *How to Become a Columnist: The Ultimate Blueprint for Guest Blogging and Syndication*. Retrieved from Buffer Social: https://blog.bufferapp.com/how-to-become-a-columnist-guest-posting-syndication

Manser, C. (2013). *Registered Users, Subscribers & Logins: What's the Difference?* Retrieved from My Second Million! How to Set Up a Blog and Make Money Online: http://www.mysecondmillion.com/register-subscribe-login/

Massenzio, D. (2015, February 14). *The Importance of an Editor and Beta Readers for Independent Authors*. Retrieved from Author Don Massenzio Blog: https://donmassenzio.wordpress.com/2015/02/14/the-importance-of-an-editor-and-beta-readers-for-independent-authors/

McGregor, J. (2015, April 17). *Amazon Pays $450,000 A Year To This Self-Published Writer*. Retrieved from

Forbes: https://www.forbes.com/sites/jaymcgregor/2015/04/17/mark-dawson-made-750000-from-self-published-amazon-books/#5985abab6b5b

McGregor, J. (2017, May 25). *Amazon Pays $450,000 A Year To This Self-Published Writer*. Retrieved from Forbes: https://www.forbes.com/sites/jaymcgregor/2015/04/17/mark-dawson-made-750000-from-self-published-amazon-books/#2779f9fc6b5b

Meyer, B. (2018, October 3). *5 Email Marketing Psychology Hacks to Boost Engagement & Sales*. Retrieved from WebEngage: https://webengage.com/blog/email-marketing-psychological-hacks/

MOZ. (n.d.). *What is SEO?* Retrieved from SEO Learning Center: https://moz.com/learn/seo/what-is-seo

Penn 01, J. (2014, October 14). *Six Figure Success Self-Publishing Non-Fiction Books With Steve Scott*. Retrieved from The Creative Penn: https://www.thecreativepenn.com/2014/10/14/non-fiction-success/

Penn 02, J. (n.d.). *My Author Timeline. From First Book To Multi-Six-Figure Author Entrepreneur*. Retrieved from The Creative Penn: https://www.thecreativepenn.com/timeline/

Pilkington, E. (2012, January 12). *Amanda Hocking, the writer who made millions by self-publishing online*. Retrieved from The Guardian:

https://www.theguardian.com/books/2012/jan/12/amanda-hocking-self-publishing

Proctor, B. (2017, September 22). Bob Proctor on How to Visualize, Think and Grow Rich & Reading | Matei Catalin YouTube video: https://www.youtube.com/watch?v=ZsrFT5WPybw. (M. Catalin, Interviewer)

Puri, R. (2015, September 16). *Content Syndication: The Definitive, Insider's Guide*. Retrieved from BuzzStream Blog: https://www.buzzstream.com/blog/content-syndication-the-definitive-insiders-guide.html

Ratcliff, C. (2016, August 3). *Search Engine Watch*. Retrieved from What is content syndication and how do I get started?: https://searchenginewatch.com/2016/08/03/what-is-content-syndication-and-how-do-i-get-started/

Samuel, L. R. (2018, February 14). *Why Do Writers Write?* Retrieved from Psychology Today: https://www.psychologytoday.com/intl/blog/psychology-yesterday/201802/why-do-writers-write

Schruers, F. (1995, July 13). *Jim Carrey: Bare Facts and Shocking Revelations*. Retrieved from Rolling Stone: https://www.rollingstone.com/culture/culture-news/jim-carrey-bare-facts-and-shocking-revelations-181569/

Singal, A. (2016). *The Circle of Profit: How to Turn Your Passion into an Information Business*. Retrieved from Lurn, Inc. (www.lurn.com):

http://circleofprofit.s3.amazonaws.com/The_Circle_of_Profit.pdf

Smith, W. (n.d.). The Mindset of High Achievers | MulliganBrothers YouTube video: https://www.youtube.com/watch?v=LhV6RItLs84&t=33s. (Unknown, Interviewer)

Smith2, W. (n.d.). Will Smith - Focus and Determination | Xeniafoon1988 YouTube video: https://www.youtube.com/watch?v=rRE_o7YWwfs. (Unknown, Interviewer)

Thompson, J. B. (2012). *Merchants of Culture: The Publishing Business in the Twenty-First Century Second Edition.* Cambridge, UK: Polity Press. Kindle Edition.

Wattles, W. D. (1910). *The Science of Getting Rich.* New York: Elizabeth Towne Publishing New York.

Winfrey, O. (n.d.). Master Class with Oprah Winfrey, Exclusive Interview | LUX4RT YouTube video: https://www.youtube.com/watch?v=9vs0zAHfI0M. (Unknown, Interviewer)

Yoast. (2018, December 24). *rel=canonical: the ultimate guide*. Retrieved from Yoast SEO for everyone: https://yoast.com/rel-canonical/

INDEX

$1,000,000 sales funnel, 121
action, 95
Adam Clarke, 31, 38, 46, 49
AirBnB, 23
Alexandra Alter, 19
Amanda Hocking, 82, 84, 169, 189
Amazon Associates, 54, 126
Amazon Author Central, 63
analysis paralysis, 131
Anik Singal, 22, 74, 81
application programming interface (API), 101
Arnold Schwarzenegger, 141, 153, 170, 180, 183
Asia, 25
Associated Press-style articles, 70
autoresponder, 81
backlink, 41
Baidu, 29
Bangkok, Thailand, 25
BETA readers, 129
Blogger, 33
Blogging Progress Reports, 123
Bob Proctor, 191
BookShots, 19, 21
bounce, 43
bounce rate, 43
Broad Match Keywords, 37
Canadian Anti-Spam Law (CASL), 77
Carol Manser, 78
Christopher Ratcliff, 62
Chuck Wepner, 162, 184
Clay Hebert, 22
click-through, 43
click-through rate, 44
Columbia, Missouri, 26
connection economy, 22, 53
contributions editor, 69
Controlling the Assault of Non-Solicited Pornography and Marketing (CAN-SPAM), 77
Disqus, 67
Don Massenzio, 129
Donald Trump, 194
Dr. Anne Bartolucci, 188
duplicate content issues, 42
earned media, 70
Eat, Pray, Love, 25
eBizMBA Guide, 63
Ed Pilkington, 82, 84
educational posts, 122
email marketing, 74

entertainment posts, 123
Entries RSS, 114
European Union (EU), 104
Exact Match Keywords, 38
expertise, authority, trust (EAT), 31, 40
Facebook, 23
faith, 95
fault lines, 94, 133
fear of missing out (FOMO), 131
featured snippets, 47
features editor, 69
Flesch Reading Ease Score (FRES), 32, 35, 49
focus group, 129
foot in the door technique, 131
General Data Protection Regulation (GDPR), 104
Google AdSense, 54
Google AdWords, 47
Google AdWords Keyword Planner, 36
Google Analytics, 36
Google Certified Professional, 38
Guglielmo Marconi, 150
Hacker News, 67
HTTP:, 45
HTTPS:, 45
Hyper Text Markup Language (HTML), 109
Indiegogo, 23
information product, 120
Infront Webworks, 46
intellectual property, 22
J. K. Rowling, 139
James Cameron, 156
James Patterson, 19, 21, 84
Jay McGregor, 76, 85
Jeff Bezos, 75
JFK, 186
Jim Carrey, 142, 143, 156, 157, 171, 172, 180, 181, 195, 196
Joanna Penn, 28, 86, 93, 123, 169
Joe Weider, 154
John B. Thompson, 60
John Fitzgerald "Jack" Kennedy, 186
Kevan Lee, 68
keyword stuffing, 30
Kickstarter, 23
Kobo Affiliates, 127
landing page, 116
LinkedIn, 63
Lisa Nichols, 144, 157, 158, 159, 163, 172, 181
Liz Schulte, 26
Lucille Ball, 156
Madonna, 149, 184, 185, 186

MailChimp for WordPress, 81
MailChimp for WordPress plug-in, 99, 100
Mark Dawson, 26, 76, 85, 120, 129, 188, 189
market research, 129
Marsha Friedman, 69
Matt Cutts, 31
META widget, 114
mobile marketing, 74
mobile-first indexing, 44
Muhammad Ali, 162, 184
Napoleon Hill, 93, 136, 178
Negative Keywords, 38
NetMarketShare, 29
OneLink, 126
Oprah Winfrey, 145, 159, 170, 171, 173, 183
opt-in, 77
opt-out, 77
organic search engine result, 30
paradox of choice, 131
pay-per-click (PPC), 38, 116
Phrase Match Keywords, 37
plotter or pantser, 52
polyphasic sleep, 194
preview audience, 129
price anchoring, 131
promotional posts, 123
psychological hacks, 124
QR codes, 108
quality traffic, 30
Quora, 27, 63
R.U. Darby, 93, 132
Really Simple Syndication (RSS), 66, 110
reciprocity, 131
Reddit, 67
rel=canonical and meta noindex tags, 42
Rhonda Byrne, 165
Ritika Puri, 68
Rocky Balboa, 162
RSS content blocks, 115
RSS Feed, 110
Sara Blakely, 140, 151, 169, 170, 178
scalability, 120
Scoop.it, 67
Search Engine Journal, 65
search engine optimization (SEO), 29
search engine spiders, 33
search quality factors, 31, 40
Searchmetrics rankings report, 31, 48
SEOBook Keyword Analyzer, 37
Seth Godin, 22
Sir Richard Branson, 193
Spanx, 140
SSL security certificates, 45
Steve Scott, 83, 84, 85
subject matter expert (SME), 23

Sylvester Stallone, 146, 161, 162, 173, 184
Terminator, 156
TheSecret.tv, 165
thought, 95
Timothy Ellis, 27
Tom Bilyeu, 158
Tony Robbins, 162
top-of-mind awareness, 71
Tumblr, 67
Uber, 23
URL (Uniform Resource Locator), 45

Wallace D. Wattles, 168, 176, 191
web crawlers, 33
website encryption, 45
WikiLeaks, 45
Will Smith, 163, 166, 167, 178
WordPress, 32
writers' conference, 26
Yoast SEO WordPress, 39
Yoast: SEO for Everyone, 50
ZergNet, 67

ABOUT THE AUTHOR

So many people are publishing books of all kinds nowadays, and they need guidance regarding best practices with everything from writing to publishing to selling those books. I've made it my life's mission to help others navigate this mysterious business littered with acronyms and peculiar old-fashioned practices.

As a bestselling author and TESOL-certified sales coach for authors with 25 years' experience in the North American English book publishing industry (in both the traditional and contemporary markets), I can show you how to write, publish, and sell your book(s) using all the effective traditional and online tricks of the trade. Add my substantial advertising sales and marketing background into the mix, and you have a serious mentor in front of you who can help you achieve commercial success as an author.

Visit my company website and blog at https://polishedpublishinggroup.com/ to download a free .PDF copy of *Profitable Publishing Today*. Here, you'll find step-by-step guidance on how to cost-effectively self-publish a successful book series.

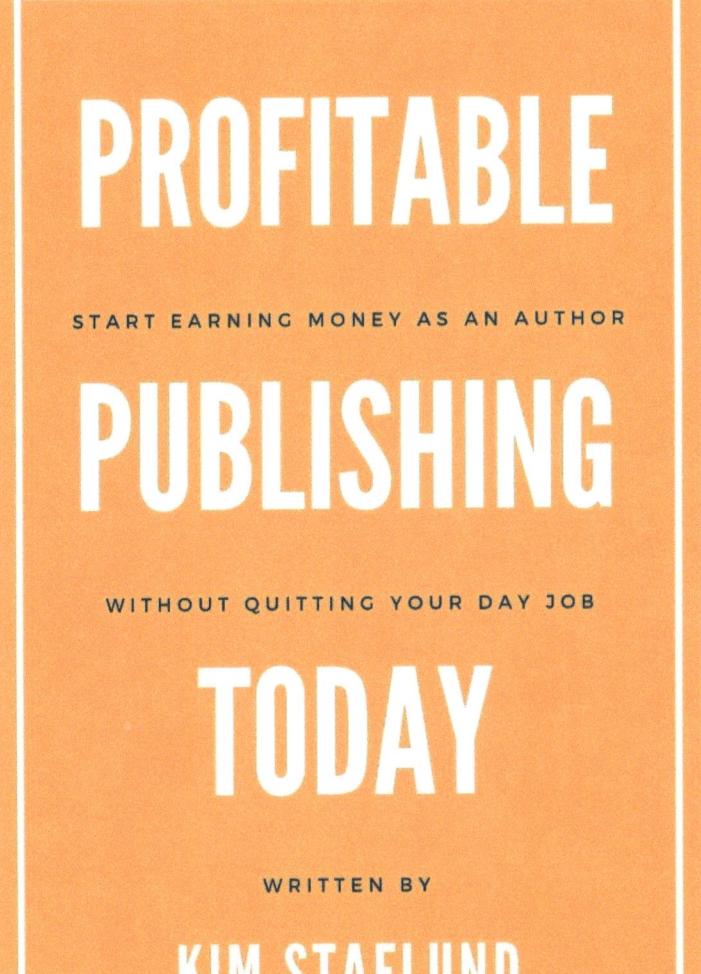

Step-by-step guidance to successful self-publishing

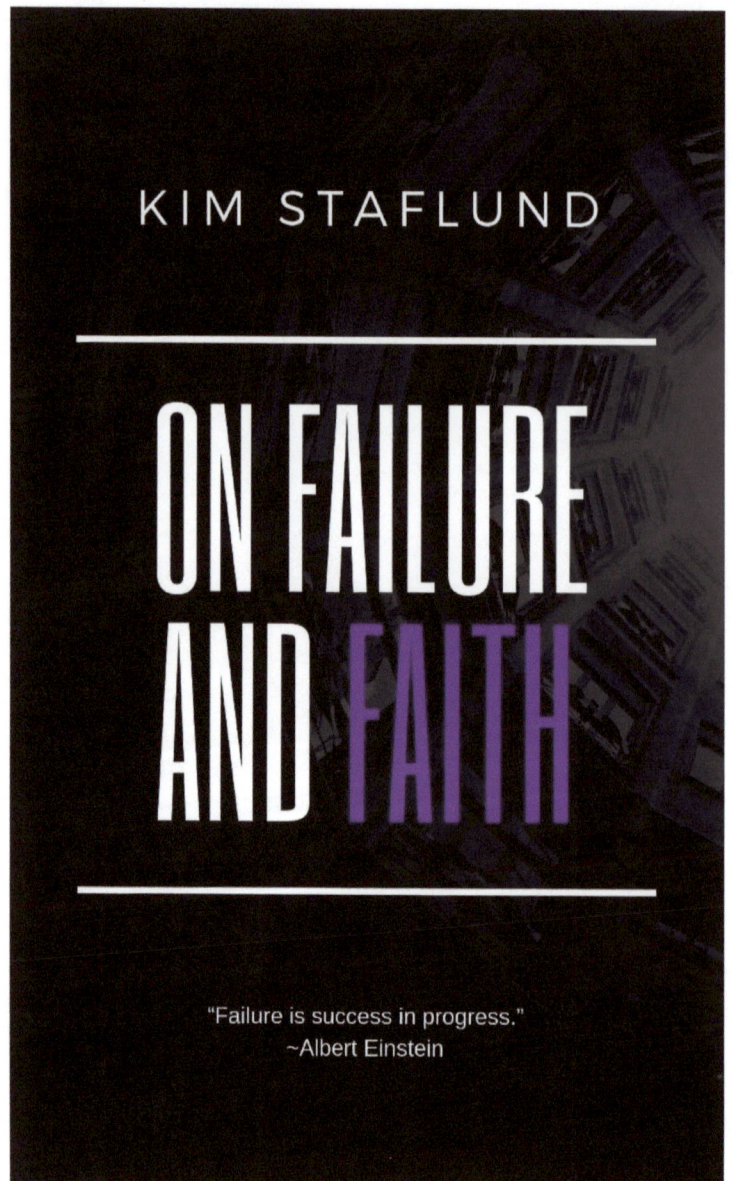

Story of what happened to me after the cliff crumbled

"Ethics is about how we meet the challenge of doing the right thing when that will cost more than we want to pay."
~The Josephson Institute of Ethics

Related Reading:

Why is Sharing Failure
More Powerful than Sharing Success?
https://polishedpublishinggroup.com/why-is-sharing-failure-more-powerful-than-sharing-success/

When is it Business and When is it Bullying?
[Snakes in Suits]
https://polishedpublishinggroup.com/when-is-it-business-and-when-is-it-bullying/

Workplace PTSD Awareness Deserves its Own Week
https://polishedpublishinggroup.com/workplace-ptsd/

www.ingramcontent.com/pod-product-compliance
Lightning Source LLC
Chambersburg PA
CBHW041610220426
43668CB00001B/3

TABLE OF CONTENTS

1 …Whipped cheesecake
5 …Buttermilk custard
9 …Carrot chiffon
15 …Key lime
19 …Roasted pears
23 …Activated charcoal crème brulee
27 …White Chocolate-Raspberry mille feuille
31 …Not Your Grandma's Apple Pie
35 …Smoked maple s'more
41 …Togarashi Pineapple Paris-Brest
45 …Greek yogurt red velvet
49 …"Dessert Street Tacos"
55 …Matcha Green Tea Flan'
59 …Twisted Ode to Elvis
63 …Caramelized raspberry shortbreads
67 …PB & J Uncrust-a-cookie
71 …Soft caramel cookie
73 …Lemonade sorbet
75 …Vanilla Bean ice cream

Whipped Cheesecake

yield: 3-5 servings

Sous Vide Cheesecake Batter

452 grams cream cheese
105 grams granulated sugar
3 grams sea salt
130 grams eggs
3 grams vanilla bean
130 grams heavy cream

Method

1. In a stand mixer with a paddle attachment, mix cream cheese, sugar, and salt until incorporated.
2. Add eggs one by one, scraping down the sides of the mixing bowl after each egg.
3. Add vanilla bean and mix until smooth and creamy.
4. Place batter in a sous vide bag, seal it, set your sous vide machine to 176 degrees F, and bake for 75 minutes.

Once batter is set and cooled, pour cream into a mixing bowl and whip until medium peaks form. Gently fold the whipped cream into the batter to create a mousse-like texture. Set aside and reserve in cooler until ready to assemble.

Potato Chips

4 fingerling potatoes, sliced
8 grams sea salt
50 grams lard, for deep frying

🍲 *Method*

1. Wash potatoes and slice with a mandoline into an ice bath.
2. Drain and rinse potatoes, then fill bowl used for ice bath with water again. Add the salt and then the potatoes. Let soak for 10 minutes. Drain potatoes into strainer and rinse again.
3. In a small pot on low heat, set lard temp to 330 degrees F.
4. Add potato slices in small batches and fry while stirring constantly, cook until light brown in color, remove with a small strainer onto paper towels, season with a dash of salt.

🫐 Blackberry Paper

116 grams fruit puree
30 grams granulated sugar

🍲 *Method*

1. In a bowl, blend puree and sugar. Spread thin onto a dehydrator tray lined with a nonstick sheet.

Dehydrate at 140 degrees F for 6 hours. Tear a piece off and place on a cool table to get cold & crispy

🍴 *Assembly*

For garnish: fresh figs, strawberries, cilantro, and crema mexicana

1. Place two small dollops of cheesecake mousse onto a plate. Garnish with fresh figs and strawberries (feel free to change up fruits *but do try it with figs and strawberries*).
2. Place a few potato chips around.
3. Place two large pieces of fruit paper on top, covering all.
4. Garnish with cilantro and crema mexicana.

Buttermilk Custard

Yield: 2-3 servings

🫕 Buttermilk Custard

250 grams heavy cream
65 grams granulated sugar
1 vanilla bean, scraped
6 grams gelatin sheets
125 grams cold buttermilk

🍳 Method

1. In a saucepan, bring cream, sugar, vanilla to a soft boil over medium heat. Remove from heat.
2. Place gelatin sheets in an ice cold water bath until soft. Squeeze out excess water. This method is called Blooming.
3. Add gelatin sheets to hot cream mixture and whisk.
4. Add buttermilk and cool down the mixture to just about room temperature. This will keep the vanilla beans from sinking to the bottom of your mold or dish.
5. Slowly pour the mixture into your mold/dish of choice and refrigerate for at least 2 hours. If you place in a mold, freeze for 2-3 hours to remove.

🫕 Compressed Watermelon

232 grams fresh watermelon, cut into small dice
29 grams extra-virgin olive oil
pinch of sea salt

🍳 Method

Place all ingredients into a sous vide bag. Set your sous vide machine to 180 degrees F for 45 minutes. Chill and reserve until ready to assemble.

🎩 Blistered Tomatoes

6 grams extra-virgin olive oil
6 baby heirloom cherry tomatoes

20 grams granulated sugar

🍲 Method

1. In a sauté pan, heat olive oil over medium heat until rippin' hot.
2. Drop tomatoes into oil and shake pan in a back-and-forth motion.
3. Sprinkle sugar over tomatoes and continue to shake pan until skins start to wrinkle. Set aside and reserve until ready to assemble.

🎩 Roasted Almonds

25 grams almonds, skin on
4 grams olive oil

pinch sea salt

🍲 Method

1. Preheat oven to 350 degrees F.
2. Toss all ingredients together on a baking sheet. Roast in oven for 10 minutes. Set aside and reserve until ready to assemble.

🎩 Mascarpone Cream

50 grams mascarpone
50 grams heavy cream
15 grams powdered sugar

🍲 Method

1. In a mixer, combine all ingredients. Beat until medium peaks form.

Assembly

For garnish: fresh mint

1. Remove custard from fridge or if removed from freezer, remove from mold and place frozen custard on dish to thaw out. Take blistered tomatoes on top in an odd-number count on 1 side
2. Pipe mascarpone cream in a staggering odd-number pattern.
3. Spoon some compressed watermelon over and garnish with roasted almonds, whole and shaved for texture. Garnish with mint.

Carrot Chiffon Cake

yield: 3-5 servings

🎂 Carrot Chiffon Cake

4 eggs, separated
50 grams extra-virgin olive oil
60 grams milk
100 grams carrot, grated fine
85 grams cake flour
3 grams baking powder
3 grams cinnamon
2 grams sea salt
2 grams cream of tartar
60 grams granulated sugar

Method

1. Preheat oven to 325 degrees F.
2. In a large bowl, whisk together egg yolks, olive oil, and milk. Add grated carrots and mix well. Set aside.
3. Sift flour, baking powder, cinnamon, and salt together, then whisk into carrot mixture to incorporate.
4. In a medium bowl, froth egg whites and add cream of tartar. Gradually add the sugar and beat until firm peaks form.
5. Gently fold together carrot mixture and meringue mixture to get a smooth batter. Pour batter onto sheet pan and bake for 25–30 minutes until it springs back when touched. (You can bake in a water bath to get a moister cake)

🎂 Candied Walnuts

2 egg whites
50 grams granulated sugar
400 grams roasted walnuts, chopped

Method

1. Preheat oven to 325 degrees F.
2. In a medium bowl, froth egg whites with sugar until soft peaks form.
3. Add walnuts and mix together.
4. Strain nuts onto sheet pan. Bake for 5–10 minutes until white, stirring every 2–3 minutes.

Pickled Carrots

500 grams unsweetened carrot juice
225 grams granulated sugar
120 grams white vinegar
6 fresh carrots

Method

1. In a saucepan, combine carrot juice, sugar, and vinegar. Bring to a soft boil over low heat.
2. Add carrots and cook in liquid over low heat until tender. Remove from liquid, Set aside.
3. Char pickled carrots on grill or hot sauté pan with a dash of olive oil.

Carrot Chips

80 grams water
100 grams sugar
1 carrot, fresh & washed

Method

1. In a saucepan, combine water and sugar. Bring to a boil over medium heat.
2. Slice carrots with a mandoline into sugar water. Blanch and dehydrate for 4 hours at 140 degrees F.

🍲 Cream Cheese Icing

452 grams cream cheese
80 grams unsalted butter
80 grams powdered sugar
300 grams heavy cream, whipped to a medium peak

🍲 Method

1. Using a paddle attachment, cream together cream cheese, butter, and sugar until smooth. Fold in whipped cream.

🍲 Carrot Gel

200 grams unsweetened carrot juice
80 grams brown sugar
cornstarch, as needed

🍲 Method

In a saucepan, combine carrot juice and brown sugar. Bring to a boil over medium heat. Thicken with a 1:1 mixture of cornstarch and water (slurry). Boil, cool, and set aside until ready to assemble.

🍲 Carrot Greens

10 carrot tops, green leafs only   pinch sea salt
150 grams olive oil, for frying

🍲 Method

1. In a skillet, heat olive oil to 330 degrees. Add carrot greens and flash-fry.
2. Set fried greens aside on a paper towel. Sprinkle with sea salt.

Assembly

1. Cut carrot chiffon into 3-by-1-inch pieces. Set each on top of 3 pieces of charred carrots.
2. Dollop some cream cheese icing onto center of chiffon.
3. Using a squeeze bottle, drizzle carrot gel onto chiffon.
4. Arrange walnuts and carrot chips along the chiffon. Garnish with fried greens.

Key Lime Pie

Yield: 4-6 servings

Lime Curd

175 grams key lime juice
335 grams granulated sugar, divided

5 whole eggs plus 4 egg yolks
160 grams unsalted butter
5 grams gelatin sheets, bloomed

Method

1. In a bowl over a double boiler, combine lime juice and half the sugar.
2. In another bowl, whisk together remaining sugar, whole eggs, and egg yolks.
3. Temper hot liquid into egg mixture slowly, whisking constantly. Return to bowl over double boiler and continue to whisk until thickened.
4. Strain mixture over butter and then add bloomed gelatin. Pipe into 1 1/2-inch PVC pipe lined with acetate or parchment paper and freeze.

Marshmallow Dust

30 grams mini marshmallows

Method

1. Dehydrate marshmallows at 140 degrees F for 12 hours. Crush into powder.

Cured Lime Segments

1 lime, segmented
80 grams granulated sugar
20 grams club soda

🍲 Method

1. Put segmented limes in a bowl, sprinkle with sugar and club soda, and toss gently.
2. Set aside and cure for 4 hours.

🍰 Teddy Graham Crumble

250 grams Teddy Grahams, crushed
200 grams unsalted butter
150 grams brown sugar
50 grams all-purpose flour

🍲 Method

1. Preheat oven to 325 degrees F.
2. In a mixer, using a paddle attachment, combine all ingredients and mix until the mixture resembles crumbs.
3. Spread on a baking sheet and bake for 7–12 minutes, until golden brown.

🍴 Assembly

For garnish: fresh raspberries and chives

1. On your dish or bowl, place 1 spoonful of Teddy Graham crumble.
2. Remove lime curd from PVC pipe and cut into 2-inch pieces. Place 2- 3" pieces on top of crumbs.
3. Arrange cured lime segments around lime curd.
4. Slice raspberries and cut chives on a bias to garnish your dish.
5. Sprinkle marshmallow dust on top and serve.

Roasted Pears

Yields 2-3 servings

🍲 Roasted Poached Pears

952 grams white grape juice
260 grams granulated sugar
3 vanilla beans
2 fresh pears, peeled, cored, and sliced
50 grams brie cheese

🍳 *Method*

1. Preheat oven to 400 degrees F.
2. In a saucepan, bring grape juice, sugar, and vanilla to a boil, then reduce to medium heat.
3. Place pear slices into hot liquid. Place parchment paper on top to submerge fruit. Cook until al dente.
4. Once pears are cooked, place onto skillet plate. Add brie and put into preheated oven. Bake until cheese is golden brown and bubbly, 6–8 minutes.

🍲 Ginger Crumble

300 grams all-purpose flour
200 grams unsalted butter
150 grams brown sugar
10 grams ginger powder
5 grams cinnamon powder
pinch sea salt

🍳 *Method*

1. Preheat oven to 325 degrees F.
2. In a mixer, using a paddle attachment, combine all ingredients and mix until mixture resembles crumbs.
3. Spread on a baking sheet and bake for 7–12 minutes until golden brown.

🍧 Green Apple Cotton Candy

6–10 pieces mini Jolly Rancher candies

🍳 *Method*

1. Place candies in a hard cotton candy machine and spin until fluffy.

🍴 Assembly

For garnish: 23 karat gold edible sheets

1. Place a spoonful of ginger crumble on plate as a base.
2. Carefully place warm roasted cheese-topped pears on the pile of crumbs. (Stop and watch the cheesy goodness pull away from the pan.)
3. Place a pile of freshly spun cotton candy on top.
4. Garnish with gold edible sheets.

Activated Charcoal Crème Brûlée

Yields 2-3 servings

Charcoal Crème Brûlée

410 grams heavy cream
50 grams half-and-half
2 vanilla beans, scraped
140 grams brown sugar
2 whole eggs plus 150 grams egg yolks
150 grams activated charcoal powder

Method

1. Preheat oven to 290 degrees F.
2. In a saucepan, combine heavy cream, half-and-half, vanilla beans, and sugar. Bring to a soft boil.
3. Meanwhile, in a large bowl, whisk together eggs and egg yolks.
4. Once cream mixture is soft-boiled, pour it over egg mixture slowly while whisking at the same time to prevent curdling.
5. Place activated charcoal powder in a bowl and strain brûlée mixture over. Blend using a stick blender or stand blender and strain.
6. On a scale, pour 160 grams into a dish of choice. Bake in a water bath for 30–35 minutes. Size of dish will determine your baking time.
7. Once baked, remove from water bath, let cool to room temperature, and then place in fridge, covered with plastic wrap.

Compressed Apple

1 Granny Smith apple, melon baller
1 piece lemongrass
29 grams apple cider

☞ *Method*

1. Place all ingredients in a vacuum-sealed bag. Drop into a sous vide water bath set to 165 degrees F for approximately 35 minutes. Set aside and cool.

🍲 Cucumber Noodles

2 fresh cucumbers, peeled
400 grams water
100 grams simple syrup
25 grams Sosa elastic

☞ *Method*

1. Blend all ingredients in a mixer or use a hand stick blender and strain into container to remove seeds.
2. Pour a thin layer onto a sheet pan and let set up in fridge. Cut into thin noodles.

🍲 Dehydrated Tomato and Beet

100 grams water
50 grams brown sugar
4 slices Roma tomato
6 slices purple beet

🥘 *Method*

1. In a saucepan, combine water and sugar and heat to create a simple syrup.
2. Gently dip each slice of tomato and beet into the simple syrup, then place onto a dehydrator mat.
3. Dehydrate at 155 degrees F for 30 hours to remove moisture and achieve a chip-like texture.

🍴 **Assembly**

For base: sugar in the raw

1. Place a layer of sugar in the raw on top of crème brûlée and caramelize evenly with a blow torch. Arrange apples pieces, beet chips, tomato chips, and cucumber noodles on top.

White Chocolate–Raspberry Mille-Feuille

Yields 2-3 servings

🍯 Caramelized Jackfruit Compote

100 grams granulated sugar, divided
250 grams coconut water
200 grams jackfruit, cleaned and chopped
cornstarch, as needed

🍲 Method

1. In a dry pan, caramelize 40 grams of the sugar. Deglaze with coconut water.
2. Once you have created a caramel coconut-water mixture, add jackfruit and remaining sugar and stir. Reduce until mixture is evaporated by half.
3. Thicken mixture with a 1:1 ration of cornstarch and water. Cook 1 minute, set aside, and cool.

🍯 Meringue Crisps

174 grams granulated sugar
87 grams corn syrup
58 grams water
116 grams egg whites

🍲 Method

1. In a saucepan, bring sugar, corn syrup, and water to a soft-ball stage, 235 degrees F.
2. Meanwhile, in a mixer, bring egg whites to a heavy froth.
3. When the sugar mixture reaches the proper stage, slowly pour into egg whites with the mixer on medium speed, then speed up to create a shiny meringues with stiff peaks.
4. Spread the mixture thin on a dehydrating silpat sheet and dehydrate for 2 hours at 155 degrees F. Break into pieces and reserve until ready to assemble.

🎒 White Chocolate Cremeaux

100 grams heavy cream
40 grams powdered sugar
50 grams egg yolks
300 grams couverture white chocolate
6 grams gelatin sheets
475 grams heavy cream, whipped to soft peaks

🍳 Method

1. In a saucepan, combine cream and sugar and heat.
2. Place egg yolks in a medium bowl. Slowly temper cream mixture into egg yolks while whisking.
3. Place chocolate in a large bowl. Strain cream mixture over chocolate.
4. Bloom your gelatin with ice water and place into warm chocolate mixture.
5. Once cooled to about room temperature, fold in whipped cream. Set aside and chill until ready to assemble.

🍳 Assembly

For layering: sliced fresh raspberries

1. Place one meringue crisp on a plate. Pipe some cremeaux on crisp. Top with a spoonful of jackfruit compote. Arrange sliced fresh raspberries on top.
2. Repeat the process for a second and third layer. Crush some dried meringue into a powder and sprinkle over as a garnish.

Not Your Grandma's Apple Pie

yield: 1-2 servings

🧂 Apple Pie Filling

116 grams butter
2 Granny Smith apples, sliced
100 grams granulated sugar
3 grams sea salt
4 grams ground black pepper
4 grams ginger powder
3 grams cinnamon powder
120 grams white cheddar cheese
116 grams dulce de leche

Method

1. In a hot pot, brown butter by cooking it until a brown nutty goodness evolves.
2. Add sliced apples and sugar. Stir to coat apple. While stirring, add salt, pepper, ginger, and cinnamon until apples are al dente and mixture is thickened.
3. Remove apple mixture from heat. Add cheddar cheese and dulce de leche. Set aside and reserve to cool.

🧂 Rustic Piecrust

580 grams flour
6 grams granulated sugar
2 grams sea salt
174 grams cold butter, cubed
116 grams cold water
58 grams Parmesan cheese powder

☞ Method

1. In a large bowl, combine flour, sugar, salt and parmesan cheese. Add cold butter and water; mix gently until mixture forms a dough.
2. Remove dough from bowl and knead gently until mixture forms a soft dough, with no crumbs left. Roll out on a floured countertop to 1/4-inch thickness.
3. Place dough in a 5-inch skillet, let extra drape over sides.

🍴 Assembly

For dusting: powdered sugar

1. Preheat oven to 400 degrees F.
2. Top dough in 4 inch skillet with apple pie filling. Fold dough over onto apples. This process does not have to be pretty; just fold it as it lies to create a rustic look.
3. Bake for 35–45 minutes until crust is golden brown. Dust with powdered sugar.

Smoked Maple S'mores

yield: 1-2 servings

🍯 Peanut Butter Custard

370 grams heavy cream
65 grams granulated sugar
1 vanilla bean, scraped
4 grams gelatin sheets, bloomed
52 grams creamy peanut butter

Method

1. In a small pot, combine cream, sugar, and vanilla. Bring to a small boil.
2. Place peanut butter in a large bowl. Pour cream mixture over peanut butter and whisk until incorporated.
3. Add gelatin to hot peanut butter mixture. Once all is incorporated and cooled, pour mixture into a mini ice cream mold, filling halfway, and freeze.

🍯 56 Percent Chocolate Mousse

100 grams heavy cream
40 grams powdered sugar
50 grams egg yolks
225 grams couverture dark chocolate
4 grams gelatin, sheets
475 grams heavy cream, whipped to soft peaks

🍲 Method

1. In a saucepan, combine cream and sugar and heat.
2. Place egg yolks in a medium bowl. Slowly temper cream mixture into egg yolks while whisking.
3. Place chocolate in a large bowl. Strain cream mixture over chocolate.
4. Bloom gelatin with ice water and add warm chocolate mixture. Once cooled to about room temperature, fold in whipped cream.
5. Pour or pipe mixture into mini ice cream mold on top of peanut butter mixture. Level off and freeze.

🔔 38 Percent Milk Chocolate Coating

600 grams couverture milk chocolate
550 grams coconut oil
125 grams corn syrup

🍲 Method

1. Place chocolate in microwave-safe bowl. Softly melt chocolate in microwave on low level.
2. Pour oil and corn syrup into chocolate and blend with an immersion blender to fully incorporate.
3. Dip frozen peanut butter/chocolate ice cream into chocolate coating mixture.

🔔 Speculoos Crumble

217 grams Speculoos biscoff cookies
60 grams unsalted butter
100 grams brown sugar
80 grams sugar
70 grams flour

🍲 Method

1. Preheat oven to 325 degrees F.
2. Crush biscoff cookies with your hands for a rough look. Set aside.
3. In a mixer, cream together butter and sugars to a smooth paste.
4. Add flour and crushed cookies and combine until mixture resembles crumbs. Spread on baking sheet and toast oven for 5–7 minutes.

🔥 Smoked Marshmallow

40 grams water
350 grams granulated sugar
225 grams smoked maple syrup
90 grams egg whites
15 grams gelatin sheets, bloomed
Spiceology honey granules

🍲 Method

1. In a small pot, bring water, sugar, and maple syrup to a soft-ball stage, 235 degrees F.
2. In a stand mixer, whip egg whites to a heavy froth or soft peak. Slowly pour in hot sugar mixture on medium speed. Add bloomed gelatin. Whip until stiff peaks form.
3. Spread honey granules on a sheet pan. Pipe marshmallow mixture over. Let set 2–4 hours.

Assembly

For garnish: toffee cashews and peanut powder

1. Put 2 tablespoons of Speculoos crumble dead center on a plate. Place the ice cream that's been dipped in chocolate on top of crumble.
2. Cut a 7-inch strip of marshmallow. Place over top of ice cream with a twist motion.
3. Pipe some of the chocolate coating on and around your dish, then add some toffee cashews to contribute some crunch. (You can find them in your local grocery store.) Dust with peanut powder. *you can purchase this though chefrubber.com or make it quickly by taking 30g peanuts & 50g of powdered sugar*

Togarashi Pineapple Paris-Brest

Yield: 3-5 servings

🍲 Togarashi Curd

5 whole eggs plus 4 egg yolks
90 grams togarashi seasoning
100 grams orange juice
75 grams mango juice
350 grams granulated sugar
40 grams unsalted butter
zest from 3 lemons

🍳 Method

1. In a large bowl, combine the eggs, egg yolks, and togarashi seasoning.
2. In a medium bowl, combine the juices and sugar. Place over a double boiler.
3. When juices are hot and sugar is fully dissolved, gently ladle juices into the egg mixture, whisking so the eggs don't curdle.
4. Pour mixture back into double boiler. Set up and whisk gently until curd starts to thicken. Remove from heat and add butter and zest. Wrap and chill.

🍲 70 Percent Chocolate Mousse

100 grams heavy cream
40 grams powdered sugar
50 grams egg yolks
225 grams couverture dark chocolate
4 grams gelatin sheets
475 grams heavy cream, whipped to soft peaks

☞ *Method*

1. In a saucepan, combine cream and sugar and heat.
2. Place egg yolks in a medium bowl. Slowly temper hot cream mixture into your egg yolks while whisking.
3. Place chocolate in a large bowl. Strain cream mixture over chocolate.
4. Bloom gelatin with ice water and place into warm chocolate mixture.
5. Once mixture is cooled to about room temperature, fold in whipped cream. Set aside and chill.

🔥 Charcoal Churro

464 grams water
100 grams unsalted butter
6 grams sea salt
12 grams granulated sugar
500 grams flour
5 grams baking powder
120 grams activated charcoal
3–4 whole eggs

☞ *Method*

1. In a saucepan, combine water, butter, salt, and sugar to a boil over medium heat. Once it reaches a boil, add flour, baking powder, and charcoal. Continue to stir until mixture becomes a paste or dough and pulls away from sides of pan. Cook for about 1 minute.
2. Place dough in a stand mixer to cool off, then slowly add eggs one by one.
3. Pipe in a circle on to a half sheet pan lined with parchment paper. Freeze for 2 hours and then fry in 350-degree F oil until fully puffed.

🍲 Pineapple Chutney

29 grams butter
40 grams brown sugar

400 grams pineapple, diced
15 grams aged balsamic vinegar

📖 Method

1. Add butter to a saucepan and start to brown. Add sugar and pineapple. Cook down into a syrup until pineapple is soft.
2. Add vinegar and cook for 2 minutes. Remove from heat and chill.

📖 Assembly

For garnish: fresh mint

1. Cut churro ring in half. Place one half on a plate. Spoon some of the chutney into the cavity and place a dollop of chocolate mousse in center.
2. Place second half of churro on top and repeat process with chutney.
3. With a pastry bag, pipe the togarashi curd in 3–4 dots per layer. Garnish with mint.

Greek Yogurt Red Velvet

Yield: 6-8 servings

🍲 Mango Puree

200 grams frozen mango chunks
60 grams granulated sugar
60 grams white cranberry juice

🍳 *Method*

1. In a saucepan, combine all ingredients and bring to a boil.
2. Reduce heat to low and heat for 3–5 minutes.
3. Puree in a blender or with an immersion blender.

🍲 Rhubarb Puree

150 grams frozen rhubarb
80 grams granulated sugar
60 grams white cranberry juice
50 grams frozen raspberries

🍳 *Method*

1. In a saucepan, combine all ingredients and bring to a boil.
2. Reduce heat to low and cook for 3–5 minutes.
3. Puree in a blender or with an immersion blender and strain.

🍲 Red Velvet Sponge

435 grams cake flour
435 grams shortening
812 grams granulated sugar
145 grams cocoa powder
51 grams milk powder
2 grams baking soda
580 grams cold water, divided

464 grams whole eggs
15 grams vanilla paste
240 grams red food coloring
200 grams greek yogurt

Method

1. Preheat oven to 350 degrees F.
2. In a mixer, combine cake flour and shortening. Cream to a smooth paste, about 3 minutes.
3. Sift together sugar, cocoa powder, milk powder, and baking soda. Add to flour mixture, scraping sides of bowl.
4. Add 232 grams water slowly, scraping sides of bowl again. Mix for 10 minutes.
5. Add eggs slowly, scraping again to prevent lumps. Mix for 4 minutes.
6. Add the vanilla, food coloring, and remaining 348 grams of water and greek yogurt. Mix for 6 minutes.
7. Spread a thin layer of batter in a sheet pan. Bake until cake springs back. Test with a toothpick.

Cream Cheese Mousseline

452 grams cream cheese
80 grams unsalted butter
80 grams powdered sugar

300 grams heavy cream, whipped to a medium peak

Method

1. In a mixer, using a paddle attachment, cream together cream cheese, butter, and sugar until smooth.
2. Fold in whipped cream.

White Chocolate Sauce

200 grams heavy cream
225 grams couverture white chocolate

☞ *Method*

1. Place cream in a microwave-safe cup. Microwave for 2–3 minutes on low level.
2. Place the chocolate in a medium bowl. Pour hot cream over and stir until incorporated.

🍴 **Assembly**

For garnish: mascarpone powder, fresh mint, and fresh raspberries.

1. Cut a 5-by-2.5-inch rectangle of sponge. Cut two holes in sponge and fill with puree sauces.
2. Place a dollop of cream cheese mousseline on sponge and dust with mascarpone powder.
3. Pipe a few placements of white chocolate sauce on sponge and on plate. Take scraps of sponge, crumble with your hands, and lace a spoonful on a corner.
4. Garnish with mint and raspberries.

DCPJ California Swag Dessert Tacos

yield: 4-6 servings

🫕 Roasted Corn Mousse

40 grams powdered sugar
575 grams heavy cream, divided
50 grams egg yolks
200 grams couverture white chocolate

4 grams gelatin sheets
2 cobs corn
butter and sugar, for grilling corn

Method

1. In a saucepan, heat powdered sugar and 100 grams of the cream.
2. Place egg yolks in a medium bowl. Slowly temper hot cream into yolks while whisking.
3. Place chocolate in a large bowl and strain cream mixture over.
4. Bloom your gelatin with ice water and add to warm chocolate mixture.
5. Grill corn until charred, rubbing with butter and sugar throughout the grilling process. This will bring out the sweetness in the corn and add a caramel flare.
6. When finished, cut the corn off the cob and puree it with the chocolate mixture. Strain to give a smooth texture. Cool to room temperature.
7. Whip remaining 475 grams heavy cream to soft peaks and fold into chocolate mixture. Set aside and chill.

🫕 Avocado Crema

2 florida avocados, pitted
30 grams sour cream
2 grams sea salt
2 grams vanilla extract
juice from 1/2 lime

Method

1. Puree all ingredients together until emulsified.

Kumquat Compote

10 fresh kumquats, sliced
80 grams orange juice
60 grams granulated sugar
1 orange, zested, peeled, and segmented
1 tablespoon cornstarch

Method

1. In a saucepan, boil kumquats in water for 2min to remove bitter oils in skin. Drain in to a strainer and then return to the saucepan, boil over low heat one more time with orange juice instead of water.
2. Add sugar, orange segments, and orange zest to kumquats and juice. Return to a boil and thicken with cornstarch and 1 tablespoon water. Boil on medium heat for 1 minute, remove by scraping into a small bowl or container and chill in refrigerator.

Roasted Corn and Dragon Fruit Salsa

2 cobs corn
butter and sugar, for grilling corn
1 fresh dragon fruit, halved
15 grams cilantro, chopped
juice from 1/2 lime
2 grams sea salt

Method

1. Grill corn until it's charred, rubbing with butter and sugar throughout the grilling process. This will bring out the sweetness in the corn.
2. Place dragon fruit halves on grill, grill-side down, for 2 minutes.
3. Cut corn off cob into a bowl. Dice dragon fruit into bowl. Add cilantro, lime juice, and salt. Reserve and chill to marinate.

Grenadine Pickled Sweet Onion

1/2 onion, sliced thin
150 grams granulated sugar
130 grams water
60 grams white vinegar
60 grams grenadine

Method

1. Slice onion thin on a mandoline and place in bowl with ice water.
2. In a saucepan, heat remaining ingredients to a soft boil over medium heat. Pour over onions.
3. Cover and pickle for 48 hours.

Brown Sugar–Tequila Pickled Radish

3 radish, fresh and sliced
150 grams granulated brown sugar
130 grams water
60 grams white vinegar
60 grams tequila
juice from 1/2 lime
2 grams sea salt

Method

1. Slice radish thin on a mandoline and place in a bowl with ice water.
2. In a saucepan, heat remaining ingredients to a soft boil over medium heat. Pour over radish.
3. Cover and pickle for 48 hours.

Corn Tortillas

232 grams masa flour
3 grams sea salt
3 grams sugar
174 grams warm water

☞ *Method*

1. In a bowl, combine flour, salt, and sugar. Slowly add water. Mix until a dough forms.
2. Knead dough and adjust with more flour and more or less water to keep it from becoming sitcky.
3. Form dough into small balls and smash with a tortilla press or another pan.

🍴 Assembly

For cooking: brown vanilla butter
For garnish: cojita cheese, fresh cilantro sprigs, and lime wedges

1. In a hot skillet, cook tortillas in brown butter with vanilla extract or vanilla beans for 1–2 minutes each side. Place tortillas in a tortilla warmer lined with paper towels.
2. Place a dollop of corn mousse on center of each tortilla. Arrange some onion, radish, kumquat compote, and salsa on top of the mousse.
3. Using a piping bag, pipe your avocado crema in three areas of the tortillas.
4. Crumble cojita cheese with your hands and spoon on as needed. Add cilantro and limes wedges for garnish.

Matcha Green Tea Flan

yield: 1-2 servings

Green Tea Flan

500 grams granulated sugar, caramelize
224 gram granulated sugar
464 grams evaporated milk
464 grams heavy cream
7 whole eggs
80 grams egg yolks, roughly 4-5 yolks
50 grams matcha green tea
1 vanilla bean, scraped

Method

1. In a saucepan, heat 500 grams of sugar and caramelize, stirring gently. Once a nice amber caramel color appears, pour evenly into ramekins.
2. Once caramel is hard, blend together remaining ingredients and strain. Pour evenly into each ramekin. Bake in a water bath at 280 degrees F for 45 minutes to 1 hour, depending on thickness of custard. Let set in fridge for 24 hours.

Mascarpone Cream

80 grams heavy cream
40 grams mascarpone
30 grams powdered sugar

Method

3. In a mixer, combine all ingredients and whip until medium peaks form.

🔔 Assembly

For garnish: green tea powder

1. Remove flan from ramekin by running a knife around the edges and gently flipping on plate; caramel will drip over everything, *yum*.
2. Cut the round edges off the flan to create a small rectangle piece of custard. Place custard in a bowl, dollop some mascarpone cream next to it, and dust some green tea powder on top.

To elevate this dish to the next level, serve with soft-boiled dulce de leche and fresh cherries.

Twisted Ode to Elvis

yield: 2-4 servings

Vanilla Toast Croutons

2 slices bread
10 grams extra-virgin olive oil
4 grams vanilla sugar

Method

1. Preheat oven to 325 degrees F.
2. Cut bread into a circle using a ring cutter. Brush both sides with olive oil and sprinkle with vanilla sugar.
3. Bake until golden brown, 3–6 minutes.

Peanut Butter Ganache

100 grams heavy cream
100 grams couverture white chocolate
50 grams creamy peanut butter

Method

1. Place cream in a microwave-safe bowl and microwave until hot on low level, 2–3 minutes.
2. Place chocolate and peanut butter in a bowl. Pour hot cream over and emulsify. Set aside at room temperature.

Brûléed Bananas

1 banana, sliced
5 grams sugar in the raw

Method

1. Sprinkle banana with sugar. Torch until caramelized.

Crispy Pancetta

500 grams lard, for frying
1- 3oz package pancetta, sliced
10 grams granulated sugar

Method

1. Heat lard to 330 degrees in a small sauce pot. Add pancetta and fry.
2. Place fried pancetta on paper towels and sprinkle with sugar.

Tempura Watercress

232 grams flour, sifted
232 grams ice-cold seltzer water
1 whole egg

Method

1. In a large bowl, whisk all ingredients into a batter. Keep cold.
2. Heat lard to 330 degrees in a small sauce pot. Add the watercress and fry.
3. Place fried watercress on paper towels.

Assembly

For piping: strawberry jam (use darbo jam, which has less water content than most jams)

1. Place 1 piece of vanilla crouton in center of plate. Pipe some of the peanut butter ganache in a circle on crouton. Place a few brûléed banana slices on ganache.
2. Break another vanilla crouton into pieces, with one going on top of ganache, side, and base.
3. In a piping bag, pipe a few dots of strawberry jam.
4. Stack pancetta on top. Garnish with a few pieces of fried watercress.

Caramelized Raspberry Shortbreads

yield: 8-10 cookies

🛍 Pâte Sablée

650 grams unsalted butter
300 grams powdered sugar
300 grams almond flour
5 grams sea salt
100 grams whole eggs
650 grams flour

🥘 Method

1. Preheat oven to 325 degrees F.
2. In a mixer, cream together butter and powdered sugar. Scrape your bowl.
3. Add almond flour and sea salt, slowly mixing until incorporated.
4. Add eggs one by one, then add flour, mixing slowly until combined into a dough.
5. Roll dough on a floured surface to a 1/4-inch thickness. Cut out circles of desired size and cut out rings. Place on a baking sheet with even space in between.
6. Bake until golden brown, 7–10 minutes. Set aside to cool.

Assembly

For sprinkling: granulated sugar and powdered sugar

For piping: strawberry jam (darbo)

1. Sprinkle granulated sugar on cookie base and torch until caramelized.
2. Place cookie rings together away from bases and sprinkle with powdered sugar.
3. Using a piping bag, pipe some jam on caramelized cookie base. Place a powdered sugar ring on top of jam to complete the cookie.

PB&J "Uncrust-a-Cookie"

Yield: 4-6 cookies

Peanut Butter Ganache

100 grams heavy cream
100 grams couverture white chocolate
50 grams creamy peanut butter

Method

1. Place cream in a microwave-safe bowl. Microwave until hot, 2–3 minutes.
2. Combine chocolate and peanut butter in a bowl. Pour hot cream over and emulsify.
3. Set aside at room temperature.

Snickerdoodle Cookies

300 grams granulated sugar, plus more for rolling
226 grams unsalted butter
2 whole eggs
13 grams vanilla paste
360 grams flour
2 grams baking soda
2 grams cream of tartar
2 grams sea salt
cinnamon, for rolling

👨‍🍳 Method

1. Preheat oven to 325 degrees F.
2. In a mixer, cream together sugar and butter lightly to form a paste.
3. Slowly add in eggs, one at a time, and vanilla, scraping the bowl.
4. In a large bowl, combine flour, baking soda, cream of tartar, and salt. Add to egg mixture in three parts until all has been added.
5. Once dough is combined, scoop into 1-inch portions, rolling into balls with your hands.
6. Place a 1:2 mixture of cinnamon to sugar in a bowl. Roll balls in mixture to coat.
7. Place balls on baking sheet, evenly spaced. Bake for 8–10 minutes.

🍴 Assembly

For sandwiches: strawberry jam

1. Pipe some peanut butter ganache around the edges of a cookie. Place some strawberry jam (I love strawberry jam, if you haven't noticed by now) in center. Put another cookie on top of PB&J mixture like a sandwich. *Eat up!*

Soft Salted Caramel Cookie

yield: 8-10 cookies

1,160 grams unsalted butter
928 grams granulated sugar, plus more for rolling
928 grams brown sugar
10 whole eggs
2,088 grams flour
15 grams baking soda
30 grams sea salt, plus more for sprinkling
1 package Nabisco caramel squares

Method

1. Preheat oven to 325 degrees F.
2. In a large bowl, mix butter and granulated sugar together until soft. Add brown sugar, scraping the bowl. Mix until incorporated.
3. Add eggs one by one until fully incorporated, scraping bowl throughout.
4. In another bowl, combine flour, baking soda, and salt. Add to sugar mixture slowly, in three parts, until fully incorporated.
5. Scoop 1-inch portions of dough and roll in your hands, then toss into a bowl of sugar. Place on cookie sheet, evenly spaced.
6. Unwrap a caramel square and shove in the center of a cookie ball. Repeat with remaining caramel squares and cookies.
7. Bake for 6 minutes. Removes pan from oven, sprinkle cookies with sea salt, and return to oven until light golden brown, 5–6 minutes for light golden brown.

No assembly needed. Eat these yummy soft cookies *warm.*

Lemonade Sorbet

yield: 2 quarts

600 grams sugar, granulated
245 grams glucose (corn syrup)
15 grams sorbet stabilizer

zest from 2 fresh lemons
3 liters lemonade
metal spoons, for serving

Method

1. In a saucepan, combine all ingredients except lemonade and heat to 181 degrees F. Rapidly cool to 40 degrees F. Place in freezer for 2–3 hours to get cold.
2. Add lemonade and run in an ice cream/sorbet machine for 25–30 minutes. Reserve in freezer.
3. Place spoons in freezer to get super cold. Once cold, place some sorbet on each spoon and serve.

Vanilla Bean Ice Cream

yield: 2 ½ quarts

500 grams milk
460 grams heavy cream, divided
200 grams granulated sugar
4 egg yolks
25 grams vanilla bean paste
3 grams sea salt

☞ Method

1. In a pot, bring milk, half the cream, and sugar to a soft boil.
2. Place egg yolks in a bowl. Slowly pour hot milk mixture over, whisking to keep egg from curdling.
3. Return mixture to pot and slowly cook to nappe stage, scraping pot with a rubber spatula back and forth until slightly thickened. *Do not overcook into an omelet*. Rapidly cool down to 40 degrees F and place in freezer for 3-4 hours.
4. Whisk in remaining cream, vanilla paste, and sea salt. Run in ice cream/sorbet machine for 45-50 minutes.

Ice cream is my favorite dessert, so I eat it right away or reserve it. Use this recipe for an à la mode on top of Not Your Grandmas Apple Pie recipe.

Think. Create. Document. Chaos. Happiness

Now that you have created your signature *Documented Chaos Pastry Journal* dishes and put your flare on them, it's time to capture your work. I love photography and taking pictures of everything because it tells a story, and stories send powerful messages, especially when it comes to food. Memories and smiles come when food is awesome (I bet you are smiling right now, thinking about food). We hold the power not only to create and play with our food but to turn someone's day into a memory they can hold and share for a lifetime. That's limitless.

One bite is all it takes to make or break a dish or a special moment. Your flavors need to shine. They need to be present at the forefront so you can close your eyes and smile.

Happiness is what my pastry journal is all about, for every baking moment you bring to the table. When you are comfortable with your abilities and bring that confidence forward, it will show in your desserts. Make dessert the cherry-on-top moment of your evening.

Think of the colors of the ingredients you are tasting. Create an idea that will complement your party, your wine, your main courses. Document everything you have done or tasted so you can go back and review your progress. Bring the chaos every time you turn on your oven. Happiness will appear when you create your *Documented Chaos* signature desserts, and especially when your guests smile. You've done it! Those are the special moments I live for.

A Chef and His Kitchen

My kitchen is for many things other than just creating and cooking. It's also my escape room for meditating, breathing, and organizing my current situation. Growing through this rugged and stressful career, I have learned to leave my crap at the door before entering the kitchen; the importance of doing so has been explained to me over and over by my chef mentors.

When I started to run my own kitchens, that's one important tool I taught my team: leave it outside, don't bring your drama into my kitchen, or you're out—it's that simple. My kitchen is my zen zone for clearing my head, focusing on the task at hand, and letting my imagination run free. I put on some loud music and, with pen and paper in hand, look around at my pantry, freezer, or walk-in for a starting point. As I taste various pieces of things, my mind works a mile a minute going through my mental bank of flavors to make these items *pop* off the map.

When I built my *Documented Chaos* test kitchen, I felt at home. This was a true reflection of myself, and a virtual fortress was all around me. This feeling can't be felt by anyone who isn't a chef, sadly. It's amazing to feel isolated at times and to let go of everything and focus 100 percent on yourself. The year 2019 marks the twelfth year of my pastry career. These years have been one hell of a road to finding my true identity as a chef. *Documented Chaos* is my kitchen to create a continuous journey.

Mise en Place

Mise en place is a French cooking term that means "putting in place" or "everything in its place." It refers to the setup you should have ready before cooking. This term has been used in professional kitchens throughout my career, and it is a helpful way to get organized. Having your recipes ready and arranging the ingredients will keep you from messing up steps or leaving out ingredients.

Properly setting up your mise en place speeds up your time management as well, so your recipes don't take an hour or two when they should take thirty minutes. Set yourself up for success by training yourself to get your mise en place straight first. Trust me, you will thank me later.

Prepare and portion out everything you need to create your *Documented Chaos* dessert, take pictures of your mise en place, and then post on your social media platforms using my hashtag #dcpjcookbookmiseneplace. Practice makes perfect!

Dehydrating

I try to bring something different to every dish I create, allowing new visuals to represent themselves. Think deep creative thoughts during this process and see what you can dehydrate. Giving ingredients a dried texture and a chip effect will elevate your dessert if used in the proper order. Dehydrating gives you the ability to bring new dimensions to your ideas.

I like to dry out ingredients after they've been prepared in a marinade or blanched or even grilled, because once dehydrated, the texture changes, and even the sweetness becomes more tart. You can dehydrate in your oven at its lowest setting of 160 degrees F, but your ingredient will get a brownish color that you don't want. For a nicer presentation, pick yourself up a dehydrator so you can get awesome, dry, crispy ingredients and even make some cool snacks like fruit leathers, chips, and additives for granola.

Equipment

Proper equipment is key to executing certain techniques for your dish—for more reasons than one. Whatever it is you want to achieve as far as texture, appearance, flavor, and smell, your dish can be brought to life through marinating, poaching, roasting, or smoking, to name just a few. While making *Documented Chaos*, I wanted to showcase some of the small equipment I use very often, not just at home but also at work for small VIP functions or events.

Sous Vide Machine

One piece of equipment I quickly fell in love with is my sous vide machine. I can marinate and poach to a certain temperature for an assigned time I want it and *boom*, done. There are some awesome ones on the culinary market now, so you have plenty of options. I currently use an Anova sous vide.

You probably noticed throughout my book that I use a sous vide machine as often as I can. Not only is this is great for making desserts, sous vide is commonly used for savory cooking to get accurate temperatures for fish and steaks or even marinating better for deeper flavors.

Mandoline

A mandoline is a must in my kitchen, even though I'm scared of this damn tool. I cut my fingertip off twelve years ago in Laguna Beach, California, while using a mandoline, and ooooooh, man. Did I feel it? Not while it was happening. I felt it afterward, but it just felt like a paper cut.

Nevertheless, I love using the mandoline as much as I can for my desserts. With its razor-sharp blades, this Japanese slicer will cut whatever you want into different thicknesses or strips. There are three interchangeable blades for setting your own style. Cutting with a knife is one alternative, but it has to be a sharp knife, and you must be very precise with your knife skills. I'm not that great at being that precise, so I use a mandoline every time.

Once you use the slicer for your ingredients, you can even use a small cookie cutter to cut shapes out of the slices for your dish. Simple things will elevate your dish on so many levels if you think of the details. All and all, it's about having fun with your food. Mom always told me "don't play with your food" … well, too late. Have fun, but be safe with your mandoline.

Tortilla Press

Growing up in Southern California, I was exposed to a diverse cultural trend of flavors, foods, spices, and smells. You name it, California has it. As I was growing up not far from Los Angeles, most street corners had taco stands known as *tacquerias*. Being around the Latin culture, I quickly picked up the name *guero*, meaning fair-skinned or white boy, or even *gringo*.

Tacos are dear to my heart, and they are a staple at my friends' and family's barbeques. My Southern California upbringing has inspired me to create my version of a street taco. Great tacos start with great masa and a solid tortilla press. I got my press from a friend of mine; his dad made it for me for my cookbook. It is so cool and easy to carry around.

Yes, I carry around my tortilla press. I take it with me house-to-house making tortillas. If you cut open a small ziplock bag, place your dough into it, and smash it down, the masa won't stick to the press and it'll stay clean. I highly suggest everyone grab a tortilla press to keep in their house or carry around like I do.

Ice Cream Maker

Who doesn't love ice cream or sorbet? I enjoy making simple, quick ice creams and fresh fruit sorbet on hot days to accompany my tacos. You can use any ice cream maker you choose, from cheap to fancy. I love my ice cream maker, and I keep the bowl frozen and ready to be locked and loaded.

You can get a quick batch out and done of ice cream or sorbet in thirty to forty-five minutes. Mix in garnishes to add texture. Experiment with flavor combinations. Make sure your bases are always super cold and chilled, though, before adding them to your machine.

What is your go-to ice cream flavor? Mine is vanilla. I use Nielsen-Massey vanilla beans for all my ice cream custard bases - hands down the best on the market and the best I've ever used throughout my twelve-year career. There are different varieties of vanilla, so choosing the right one for your flavor profile is ideal. Check 'em out, do some homework on vanilla beans, and be ready to be amazed.

Food Saver

Instead of wrapping all the food I need to save in plastic wrap, I picked up a food saver for my house close to two years ago, and *wow*, man. I use this for all my scraps—chopped herbs, veggies, proteins, fruits, flour, sugar, etc.

Saved food can be used with your sous vide machine. Vaccum-seal it and place it in a water bath at a set temperature. The food saver I have has a hose attached to it. It uses special bags that look like a ziplock but have circular grooves where you attach the hose to extract the air. It's supercool!

www.ingramcontent.com/pod-product-compliance
Lightning Source LLC
Chambersburg PA
CBHW041611220426
43668CB00001B/9